CW00553238

THE
ART OF
GOLF

OLEANDER PRESS

The Oleander Press
16 Orchard Street
Cambridge
CB1 1JT

www.oleanderpress.com

First published: 1887
Second edition: 1892
This edition published by the Oleander Press: October 2008

ISBN: 9780906672877

Designed and typeset by Hamish Symington • www.hamishsymington.com

Printed in England by Antony Rowe Ltd, Chippenham.

"Sacred to hope and promise is the spot."

"Pleasures are more beneficial than duties, because, like the quality of mercy, they are not strained, and they are twice blest."

R. L. S.

TO

THE HONOURABLE COMPANY

OF EDINBURGH GOLFERS

THIS BOOK IS DEDICATED

HUMBLY AS A GOLFER

PROUDLY AS THEIR CAPTAIN

GRATEFULLY FOR MERRY MEETINGS

AND

CORDIALLY WITHOUT PERMISSION

BY

THE AUTHOR.

Introductory Note

The Art of Golf is a most interesting book and shows how little golf and its technique have changed over the years since it was first published. Yes, the equipment looks very different, the clothes archaic, but it's a game still played sideways on, with intelligent people hitting a ball over four miles in an effort to put it into a hole $4\frac{1}{2}$ inches across!

The words in this book may be ancient, but there are one or two very interesting observations that are still viable to this day. A pleasant, enjoyable historical read about the game of golf.

Peter Allis
October 2008

Preface to the First Edition

A Preface would be superfluous were it not necessary to say a word or two about the Illustrations. My aim was to show (for the first time, I believe), by means of instantaneous photography, the movements made by players with a classical style in the process of striking a golf ball. For plates in this book (with the exception of Nos. XII, XIII, XVII and XVIII, which are the work of Mr Alexander Nicol, Photographer) I have to, and do, cordially thank my friend Mr A. F. Macfie, whose knowledge of the game, and whose skill with the camera, have enabled him to catch movements which are in many cases so swift as to escape ordinary observation. That the illustrations, therefore, truly represent the styles of the fine players who stood for them, no reader need doubt.

The authority of the text is another matter. It may be – nay, it has been – asked, 'What does he know about it?' Indeed (and alas!) I cannot speak from the highest platform. But if a poor cricketer, a hopeless billiard player, an execrable shot, begins golf by the doctor's orders after three decades, flounders hopelessly for years, and then by theory and experiment evolves a golf which I shall only characterise as infinitely better than his cricket, his billiards, or his shooting ever were, it is evident that he knows (whether he can say it) something of that department of brick-making which does not depend upon the qality of the straw.

3 Belgrave Crescent, Edinburgh
May 1887

Contents

Part Two: Of Playing the Game

OUT OF FORM

Illustrations

PART ONE

Preliminary, and Principally Foolish

CHAPTER ONE

The Praise of Golf

THERE ARE SO many good points about the royal and ancient game of golf that its comparative obscurity, rather than its increasing popularity, is matter for wonder. It is apparently yet unknown to the Medical Faculty. The golfer does not find it in the list of exercises recommended by doctors to persons engaged in warfare with the results of sedentary habits. He is moved to pity British subjects compelled to stir their livers by walking, horse-riding, or cycling. He knows how monotonous it is following one's nose, or flogging a horse and following it, compared with flogging and following a ball. For the wearied and bent cyclist, who prides himself on making his journey in as short a time as possible, he has a pitying word. Men who assume that the sooner the journey is over the greater the pleasure, evidently do not love their pursuit for its own sake. With any other sport or pastime golf compares favourably.

With Cricket? The golfer has nothing to say against that game, if you are a good player. But it is a pastime for the few. The rest have to hang about the pavilion, and see the runs made. With the golfer it is different. He does not require to be even a second-class player, in order to get into matches. Again, the skilful cricketer has to retire when he gets up in years. He might exclaim with Wolsey: 'Had I served my golf as I have served my cricket, she would not thus have deserted me in my old age.' How different it is with golf! It is a game for the many. It suits all sorts and conditions of men. The strong and the weak, the halt and the maimed, the octogenarian and the boy, the rich and the poor, the clergyman and the infidel, may play every day, except Sunday. The late riser can play comfortably, and be back for his rubber in the afternoon; the sanguine man can measure himself against those who will beat him; the half-crown seeker can find victims, the gambler can bet, the man of high principle, by playing for nothing, may enjoy himself, and yet feel good. You can brag, and lose matches; depreciate yourself, and win them. Unlike the other Scotch game of whisky-drinking, excess in it is not injurious to the health.

Better than fishing, shooting, and hunting? Certainly. These can only be indulged in at certain seasons. They let you die of dyspepsia during the rest of the year. Besides, hunting, you are dependent on horses and foxes for sport; shooting, on birds; fishing, on the hunger of a scaly but fastidious animal. The pleasures of sport are extracted from the sufferings of dumb animals. If horses, grouse or fish could squeal, sports would be distressful rather than amusing.

Golf has some drawbacks. It is possible, by too much of it, to destroy the mind; a man with a Roman nose and a high forehead may play away his profile. That peculiar mental condition called

'Fifish' probably had its origin in the east of the Kingdom. For the golfer, Nature loses her significance. Larks, the casts of worms, the buzzing of bees, and even children, are hateful to him. I have seen a golfer very angry at getting into a bunker by killing a bird, and rewards of as much as ten shillings have been offered for boys maimed on the links. Rain comes to be regarded solely in its relation to the putting greens; the daisy is detested, botanical specimens are but 'hazards,' twigs 'break clubs.' Winds cease to be east, south, west, or north. They are ahead, behind, or sideways, and the sky is bright or dark, according to the state of the game.

A cause of the comparative obscurity of golf is that the subject cannot easily be treated by the novelist. Golf has no Hawley Smart. Its Whyte Melville did not write, but played. You can ride at a stone wall for love and the lady, but what part can she take in driving at a bunker? It is natural that Lady Diana should fall in love with Nimrod when she finds him in the plough, stunned, broken-legged, the brush, which he had wrested from the fox as he fell, firm in his lifeless grasp. But if Beauty found us prone on the putting green, a $27\frac{1}{2}$ embedded in our gory locks, she might send us home to be trepanned; but nothing could come of it, a red coat notwithstanding. No! at golf ladies are simply in the road. Riding to hounds and opening five-barred gates, soft nothings may be whispered, but it is impossible at the same moment to putt and to cast languishing glances. If the dear one be near you at the tee, she may get her teeth knocked out, and even between the *shots* arms dare not steal round waists, lest the party behind should call out 'fore!' I have seen a golfing novel indeed; but it was in manuscript, the publishers having rejected it. The scene was St. Andrews. He was a soldier, a statesman, an orator, but only a seventh-class golfer. She, being St. Andrews born, naturally preferred a rising player. Whichever of the two made the best medal score was to have her hand. The soldier employed a lad to kick his adversary's ball into bunkers, to tramp it into mud, to lose it, and he won; but the lady would not give her hand to a score of 130. Six months passed, during which the soldier studied the game morning, noon and night, but to little purpose. Next medal-day arrived, and he was face to face with the fact that his golf, unbacked by his statesmanship, would avail him nothing. He hired and disguised a professional in his own clothes. The ruse was successful; but alas! The professional broke down. The soldier, disguised as a marker however, cheated, and brought him in with 83. A three for the long hole roused suspicion, and led to inquiry. He was found out, dismissed from the club, rejected by the lady (who afterwards made an unhappy marriage with a left-handed player) and sent back in disgrace to his statesmanship and oratory. It was as good a romance as could be made on the subject, but very improbable.

Although unsuited to the novelist, golf lends itself readily to the dreaming of scenes of which the dreamer is the hero. Unless he is an exceptionally good rider, or can afford 300 guinea mounts, a man cannot expect to be the hero of the hunting-field. The sportsman knows what sort of shot he is, and the fisher has no illusions; but every moderately good golfer, on the morning of the medal-day, may lie abed and count up a perfect score for himself. He easily recalls how at different times and often he has done each hole in par figures. Why not this day, and all the holes consecutively? It seems so easy. The more he thinks of it the easier it seems, even allowing for a few mistakes. Every competitor who is awake soon enough sees the necessity for preparing a speech against the contingency of the medal being presented to him in the evening. Nor is anyone much crushed when all is over, and he has not won. If he does well, it was but that putt, that bad lie, that bunker. If his score is bad, what of it? Even the best are off their game occasionally. Next time it will be different. Meanwhile his score will be taken as a criterion of his game, and he is sure to win many half-crowns from unwary adversaries who underrate him.

The game of golf is full of consolation. The long driver who is beaten feels that he has a soul above putting. All those who cannot drive thirty yards suppose themselves to be good putters. Your hashy player piques himself on his power of recovery. The duffer is a duffer merely because every second shot is missed. Time or care will eliminate the misses, and then! Or perhaps there is something persistently wrong in driving, putting, or approaching. He will discover the fault, and then! Golf is not one of those occupations in which you soon learn your level. There is no shape or size of body, no awkwardness nor ungainliness, which puts good golf beyond one's reach. There are good golfers with spectacles, with one eye, with one leg, even with one arm. None but the absolutely blind need despair. It is not the youthful tyro alone who has cause to hope. Beginners in middle age have become great and, more wonderful still, after years of patient duffering, there may be a rift in the clouds. Some pet vice which has been clung to as a virtue may be abandoned, and the fifth-class player burst upon the world as a medal-winner. In golf, whilst there is life there is hope.

It is generally agreed that the keenest pleasure of the game is derived from long driving. When the golfer is preparing to hit a far clean straight shot, he feels the joy of the strong man that rejoiceth to run a race; that is to say, the joy we have authority for believing that the Jewish runner felt. The modern sprinter experiences none. On the contrary, there is the anticipation, through fatigue, of as much pain as if he were ringing the dentist's door-bell. For the golfer in the exercise of his strength there is neither pain nor fatigue. He has the combined pleasures of an onlooker and a performer. The blow once delivered, he can stand at ease and be admired whilst the ball makes the running.

There is no such being as a golfer uninterested in his driving. The really strong player seems to value his least; but this is merely because so many of his shots are good that they do not surprise him. Let it, however, be suggested that some other is a longer driver than he, and the mask of apathy will at once fall from his face, his tongue will be loosened, and he will proceed to boast. Even when a man cannot feel that he drives quite as far as the best, his pride in his own frame in not necessarily destroyed, as by most other sports. The runner, the jumper, the lifter of weights, even the oarsman, is crushed down into his true place by the brutal rudeness of competitive facts. Not so the golfer. A. says, 'I drive with a very light club, therefore admire my strength.' B. smiles complacently, whilst you marvel at the heaviness of his – a brawny muscular smile. Little C.'s club is nearly as long as himself. The inference is that little C.'s garments cover the limbs of a pocket Hercules. D. can drive as far with a cleek as common men with a club. D. is evidently a Goliath. The inferences may be all wrong. A. may be a scrag, C. a weed, D. merely beefy. On the other hand, each may be what he supposes himself. This is one of the glorious uncertainties of the game.

To some minds the great field which golf opens up for exaggeration is its chief attraction. Lying about the length of one's drives has this advantage over most forms of falsehood, that it can scarcely be detected. Your audience may doubt your veracity, but they cannot prove your falsity. Even when some rude person proves your shot to be impossibly long, you are not cornered. You admit to an exceptional loft, to a skid off a paling, or, as a last appeal to the father of lies, you may rather think that a dog lifted your ball. 'Anyhow,' you add conclusively, 'that is where we found it when we came up to it.'

CHAPTER TWO

The History of Golf

G OLF, BESIDES being a royal game, is also a very ancient one. Although it cannot be determined when it was first played, there seems little doubt that it had its origin in the present geological period, golf links being, we are informed, of Pleistocene formation.

Confining ourselves to Scotland, no golfer can fail to be struck with the resemblance to a niblick of the so-called spectacle ornament of our sculptured stones.

Many antiquarians are of the opinion that the game did not become popular till about the middle of the 15th century. This seems probable, as in earlier and more lawless times a journey so far from home as the far-hole at St. Andrews would have been exceedingly dangerous for an unarmed man.

It is not likely that future research will unearth the discoverer of golf. Most probably a game so simple and natural in its essentials suggested itself gradually and spontaneously to the bucolic mind. A shepherd tending his sheep would often chance upon a round pebble, and, having his crook in his hand, he would strike it away;

for it is as inevitable that a man with a stick in his hand should aim a blow at any loose object lying in his path as that he should breathe.

On pastures green this led to nothing; but once on a time (probably) a shepherd, feeding his sheep on a links – perhaps those of St. Andrews – rolled one of these stones into a rabbit scrape. 'Marry,' he quoth, 'I could not do that if I tried' – a thought (so instinctive is ambition) which nerved him to the attempt. But man cannot long persevere alone in any arduous undertaking, so our shepherd hailed another, who was hard by, to witness his endeavour. 'Forsooth, that is easy,' said the friend and trying failed. They now searched in the gorse for as round stones as possible, and, to their surprise, each found an old golf ball, which, as the reader knows, are to be found there in considerable quantity even to this day. Having deepened the rabbit scrape so that the balls might not jump out of it, they set themselves to practising putting. The stronger but less skilful shepherd, finding himself worsted at this amusement, protested that it was a fairer test of skill to play for the hole from a considerable distance. This being arranged, the game was found to be much more varied and interesting. They had at first called it 'putty,' because the immediate object was to putt or put the ball into the hole or scrape, but at the longer distance what we call driving was the chief interest, so the name changed to 'go off,' or 'golf.' The sheep having meantime strayed, our shepherds had to go after them. This proving an exceedingly irksome interruption, they hit upon the ingenious device of making a circular course of holes, which enabled them to play and herd at the same time. The holes being now many and far apart, it became necessary to mark their whereabouts, which was easily done by means of a tag of wool from a sheep, attached to a stick, a primitive kind of flag still used on many greens almost in its original form.

Since these early days the essentials of the game have altered but little. Even the styme must have been of early invention. It would naturally occur as a quibble to a golfer who was having the worst of the match, and the adversary, in the confidence of three or four up, would not strenuously oppose it.

That golf was taken up with keen interest by the Scottish people from an early day is evidenced by laws directed against those who preferred it to archery and church-going. This state of feeling has changed but little. Some historians are however, of opinion that during the seventeenth century golf lost some of its popularity. We know that the great Montrose was at one time devoted to it, and that he gave it up for what would now be considered the inferior sport of Covenanter-hunting. It is also an historical fact that Charles I actually stopped in the middle of a game on Leith Links, because, forsooth, he learned that a rebellion had broken out in Ireland. Some, however, are of opinion that he acted on this occasion with his usual cunning – that at the time the news arrived he was being beaten, and that he hurried away to save his half-crown rather than his crown. Whatever the truth may be, it is certain that anyone who in the present day abandoned a game because the stakes were not sufficiently high would be considered unworthy of the name of a golfer.

The rest of the history of the game, is it not written in Mr Clark's book?

CHAPTER THREE

The Nature of the Game

GOLF BELONGS to that large class of human games in which a ball plays the principal part. Balls of all sorts and sizes amuse men – hard ones, soft ones, large ones, small ones. These are treated in a variety of ways. They are struck, used to strike with, pushed against each other, knocked into holes, rolled as close as possible to things, battered against walls, knocked over nets, cuffed with the hand, jerked with the finger and thumb, struck with an instrument, kicked with the feet, etc. In some games the ball is buffeted whilst in motion, in others whilst at rest. In some, one player's aim is to make it go whilst others try to stop it, or both may want to keep it moving, each hoping that the other will fail to do so. In games where it is the adversary's object to stop the ball, he keeps his face towards it and catches it with his hands; when he loses by doing so his back is turned, and he runs (except in war, in which the adversary does not wish to be struck, but should nevertheless have his face to the ball). In some games there is but one ball, about which there is a continual struggle; in others, each has it alternately. There is a common element in them all – rivalry.

Now golf is a game in which each player has a small hard ball of his own, which he strikes with a stick whilst it is quiescent, with the intention of putting it into a hole. Abstractly he wishes to do this with as few blows as possible, concretely in fewer than his opponent. A round of the green is called a match. A match is the best of nine, twelve, or eighteen games. Each game is called a hole, because it ends at the bottom thereof. The tee is not, as in many other games, the object aimed at, but the point started from. It consists of a small pile of sand placed on the ground, and solidified by the palm of the hand. On this the ball is placed. Each blow or miss is called a stroke, that is to say – a stroke is constituted purely by intention. A stroke is not the same thing as a rub, which is usually a blow received by a third party, but it is nearly identical with a shot. The latter, however, does not include a miss in the same impartial way as the former.

The distance between the tees and the holes is from a hundred to five hundred yards. After leaving the tee, you are not allowed to do anything to the ball except strike it or swear at it until you have either given up the hole or got to the bottom of it. In each hole there is a flag, so that its whereabouts may be seen from a distance. This is temporarily removed when the player gets near it. The flags are little bits of cloth or a bunch of wool at the end of a stick or wire; but on greens where they are not habitually stolen, the whole flag is of iron, with the name and number of the hole printed on the top. These names are for the most part either geographical, personal, gastronomical, or arithmetical. The geographical names are suggested by peculiarities of the

ground around or in front of the hole. If there are none, a wall
or a bathing-machine in the neighbourhood may suggest a name.
Holes called after people have usually been planned, laid out, and
added to the course by their godfathers, who for the first ten years
earn anything but gratitude, as these new holes are for a long time
very rough and bad; a public-house or a refreshment-stall in the
neighbourhood of a hole is always recognised as its most important feature, and it is christened accordingly. The last hole is called
the last, the one at the extremity of the links the far-hole, unless a
public-house be there to make such a consideration unimportant;
for it is admitted on all hands that the state of a man's stomach
has much to do with his game.

The grounds on which golf is played are called links, being
the barren sandy soil from which the sea has retired in recent
geological times. In their natural state links are covered with long,
rank benty grass and gorse. These get worn away by sheep and
golfers, and short springy sandy turf is disclosed. The part of the
links thus worn is the course. Links are too barren for cultivation;
but sheep, rabbits, geese, and professionals pick up a precarious
livelihood on them. A good course ought to be from 50 to 100
yards wide, the ground undulating or even hilly. The finer the
turf is the better; but it is never perfect, because golfers are always
slicing bits of it out with their clubs, quicker than the green-keeper
can replace them, which is not saying much. When you find your
ball lying on one of these scrapes, you bemoan; but it is only when
breaks in the turf are found within twenty yards of the hole that
the green-keeper is inexcusable.

On every course there ought to be plenty of hazards – that is, places where a shot is lost unless the driving be far enough, straight, or high. Off the course there are rabbit-holes, gorse bushes, railways, ploughed fields, gardens, and green-houses for crooked drivers; on it, bunkers or sand-holes for topped and short balls. The best kind of bunkers are natural. Those which are often visited usually have names, being called some man's nose or grave, or merely his bunker. To have a bunker named after you is a *monumentum aere perennius*. People like being godfathers to bunkers, although it is not usually complimentary to their driving. Where there is a lack of natural bunkers, artificial ones are dug. Walls, roads, ditches, and copses serve as hazards on the course, but these are not recognised as so desirable as bunkers.

CHAPTER FOUR

Of Sets of Clubs and other Golfing Appurtenances

A SET OF clubs may be defined as that assortment which the player's caddy carries in a cover on wet days. On fine days the player carries one club himself, either that which he has just used or the one he is about to employ.

I propose here to give a descriptive list of all the clubs which may or may not be in a set.

Nearly everyone carries a play club, an instrument consisting of many parts. It has no legs, but a shaft instead. It has, however, a toe. Its toe is at the end of its face, close to its nose, which is not on its face. Although it has no body, it has a sole. It has a neck, a head, and clubs also have horns. They always have a whipping, but this has nothing to do directly with striking the ball. There is little expression in the face of a club. It is usually wooden; sometimes, however, it has a leather face. Clubs, without being clothed, occasionally have lead buttons, but never any button holes. Clubs' heads are some black, some yellow, but colour is not due to any racial difference. From this description it will be easy to understand, without a diagram, what a club is like.

Spoons in most respects resemble clubs. Their faces are somewhat more open. There are long, short, and mid spoons, so called according to the length of the spoon.

Brassies differ from spoons and play clubs in that they have brass bottoms which are screwed on.

Irons and cleeks have no sole. Their toes and noses are one and the same thing. They have iron faces. They are never whipped. They have sockets instead of necks. Their mode of locomotion is called 'approaching.' This is a short swinging gait. Sometimes, like play clubs, they drive, but no kind of club ever walks. There are different kinds of irons. A driving iron is used when it is too far to go without doing so. Lofting irons are more light-headed; they look like their work, but do not always do it. Cleeks are cleeks; they are not marked out from their creation for special uses. You may carry a driving and an approaching cleek, and a cleek for putting; but if someone steals your set, or if you die, your putting cleek may be used for driving, etc. etc.

Then there are putters. A good one ought to have the name 'Philp' stamped on it by somebody who must not tell you that he did it himself, or it must have belonged to someone else before you got it – either an old golfer who is dead (no matter whether he was a good holer-out or not) or else to a professional. No golfer with any self-respect uses a putter which he has bought new out of a shop for four shillings.

The niblick is too vulgar-looking for description in a polite treatise like this. He is a good fellow, however, ever ready to get you out of a hole.

These are the ordinary clubs, but there are many more. There are clubs with vulcanite heads, with German silver faces, with horn faces, clubs with bamboo shafts, clubs with cork grips. Old gentlemen use baffy spoons.

The 'President' is a niblick with a hole in it, which might be a very good niblick if it were not a president. It is called a president because the hole makes it clear-headed. There are putting irons which are not irons but putters. People who putt badly use these, and are happy, although they only put it out of their power ever to putt well. There are putters made like croquet mallets, and there are perfectly upright ones. The latter are of no use to corpulent persons, as they cannot see the ball. Even the emaciated hole-out better without them.

Old-fashioned irons look like the missing link between a meat cleaver and a kitchen spoon. They all originally belonged to some-body's grandfather, and are only now to be found in glass cases or in the sets of very bad players, who, according to whether they had a golfing grandfather or not, expiscate or purchase them. The player, when getting this instrument from his caddy, does not ask for an iron in the usual way. He says 'Give me *my* heavy iron,' in a tone which causes the inexperienced adversary to despair. In reality, using an old-fashioned iron is the last expedient of those who cannot loft a ball with anything else. Even this expedient often fails, but defeat is at least avenged by the destruction of the green.

In addition to ordinary and extraordinary, there are special clubs (most of my own invention), few of which have as yet come into general use.

The automatic self-adjusting tee is a simple little contrivance whose name explains it. It prevents toeing, heeling, and topping, correcting errors in the swing of the club, acting somewhat in the same way as the compensating balance of a watch. It is a convenience to attach the automatic tee to your button-hole by a string which can be used to lift it to your hand after each shot, just as the organ-man jerks up his monkey when about to move on.

The portable platform for the feet, when the stance is bad, cannot be recommended. A spade to level the ground is more easily carried, and equally efficacious.

The 'Dynamite' is a very powerful weapon. It is a club in the face of which is inserted a small cartridge which explodes when the ball strikes it. With this club a good driver has been known to get past the long hole at St. Andrews in one shot. Loading for each drive is, however, so inconvenient that the dynamite has not come into general use. Besides, the trouble, the expense, and danger connected with it are so considerable as to make it unpopular. It would be rash to start on a round without a surgeon to carry the clubs, and surgeons of course charge more than ordinary caddies. If dynamites came into general use the rules of golf would require to be slightly altered. As they stand at present, holes would occasionally be lost because the player could not come up to time. Ten minutes is scarcely enough to allow for trepanning, which would often be necessary, as the cartridge frequently fails to go off till the club has reached the level of the head. With a dynamite it is safer to jerk than to take a full swing. The author does not recommend the dynamite. It reduces golf too nearly to the level of grouse driving or covert shooting.

The putter scale is a light iron tripod, into which you adjust an ordinary putter, placing the tripod so that the head of the putter rests behind the ball. On the tripod there is a scale showing the distance the putter is to be drawn back and let fall for each length of putt. Of course the player has to guess the said length for himself.

We now come to the subject of golf balls, of which, as of clubs, there are many kinds – not, however, like the clubs, to be used for different shots. There are twenty-sixes to twenty-nines, guttas, eclipses, black, white, and red balls, and the magnet ball. The numbers twenty-six to twenty-nine are purely sentimental. White balls are used when there is neither snow nor daisies, red ones when there is either, black ones by the poor and the stingy. Black eclipses are less objectionable than black guttas, for at least they are round. With a black eclipse one is allowed to pretend that the love of money is not the root of the evil. The magnetic ball is one of my own many inventions. It is simply an ordinary ball containing a small magnet which enables the player to hole-out with great precision, the iron in the hole (the 'tin,' it is called) attracting the magnet. For driving north the magnet ball is very good, but in driving east or west some allowance must be made for the skid of attraction. During a thunderstorm the carry of these balls is really astonishing.

'But,' cries the beginner despondingly, 'must I buy all these things?' He certainly may if he choose. Like some patent medicines, if they do no good, they will do no harm. The usual course, however, for the tyro is reluctantly to be persuaded to buy a cleek and a driver, and to get the loan of a ball. This is sure to decide him to go in for the game, and he buys a full set – namely a driver, a long spoon, a mid spoon, a short spoon, a cleek, an iron niblick, a putter, if he goes to a club-maker. If he buys a friend's spare clubs, they will be a more necessitous-looking lot, the shafts either twisted or too thick to twist. This does not much matter, as the whole set will be broken several times over before the tyro begins to develop notions of his own. With an old coat, nailed boots, and some balls, he is ready to start. Gloves for blistered hands, pitch to make the gloves grip, sticking-plaster for frayed fingers, a knife for sharp nails, elastic wristlets for started sinews, may be purchased either at once or as the necessity for them arises. As soon as the tyro is admitted to a club, it is his duty to buy a golfing umbrella for the use of the members.

Bad players always carry a very large set, but the converse of this proposition is not true, many good ones doing the same. Still, there are certain inferences to be drawn from sets of clubs. One need never be afraid to give a shade of odds to a player who carries three spoons. It is safer not to bet with a man who has none. Why bad players carry all these spoons I have never been able to make out. Perhaps it is to encourage themselves with – to use and discard as each in rotation proves itself ineffectual. It is certain that one or other becomes for the time being favourite. It is the best club he ever had; he can drive further with it than with a play club (a doubtful advantage, one would think. Would a man praise a putter which sent a two-yard putt three past the hole?). The largeness of a bad player's set is usually due to excess of wooden clubs. Approaching, being all a fluke, he leaves to chance. The good player with notions, on the other hand, runs riot in irons and cleeks, mashies, niblicks and putters, each of which is supposed to have specialties in the way of loft, length of carry, etc. etc. That constantly changing does not ruin his play is because of the extra care needed to hit accurately. The man of one iron is apt now and then to miss from too implicit trust in the familiar face which has never deceived him for many a round.

CHAPTER FIVE

Of Caddies

CADDIES ARE persons employed to carry golfers' clubs. Some people call them 'caudies,' others try to do without them; but experience teaches that a bad one is better than none. On the older greens, where carrying is established as a free trade, there is a very miscellaneous selection of caddies – boys, ragamuffins just out of prison, workmen out of a job, and professional carriers. All but the last ought to be avoided.

A good boy to carry is not a bad thing in its way. From him too much must not be expected. If the tees he makes are not over two inches in diameter, if each time a club is required he is not further than three minutes' walk from his master, if he knows the names of the clubs, he is a good boy. But on free greens, where there are professionals, the boys do not come up to this standard. They are, however, cheaper than professionals. The workman out of a job is not cheaper, besides being more inefficient than a boy.

From men who have adopted carrying as a trade, the golfer is entitled to expect the highest standard of efficiency. If he carries for you regularly, the professional ought to know what club you intend to take, and to give it without being asked. When you are in doubt about how to play your shot, he ought to confirm you in the opinion you have formed regarding it. He must never show the just contempt he has for your game.

Carrying clubs is one of the most agreeable trades open to the lower orders. In it an amount of drunkenness is tolerated which in any other would land the men in the workhouse. A very low standard of efficiency and very little work will secure a man a decent livelihood. If he is civil, willing to carry for three or four hours a day, and not apt to drink to excess before his work is done, he will earn a fair wage, and yet be able to lie abed till nine in the morning like a lord. If he does not drink (this is a hard condition, as he has little else to do), he is positively well-off; if he makes balls, and can play a good game himself, he may become rich. A caddy who, in addition, employs his leisure (of which there will still remain a great deal) in acquiring the elements of an education, may rise to be a green-keeper or a club-master, and after his death be better known to fame than many a defunct statesman or orator.

As a rule, however, the professional caddy is a contented being, spending what he gets as soon as he gets it, a Conservative in politics, a heathen in religion. He is a Conservative because he likes and admires gentlemen, who, according to his idea, are the class which plays golf and overpays him. He is a heathen, churches being to his mind as sacred to gentlemen as clubs.

A caddy's occupation being connected with a sport, he hates anything which would tend to make it a steady, regular wage-earning business. Accordingly badges, tariffs, and benefit societies he abominates. Clubs or eating-houses got up for his advantage he will have nothing to do with, if conditioned with the payment of a periodical sum, however small. A coffee-house erected for him unconditionally is well enough. It can do no more harm than the gift of a suit of old clothes too ragged to wear. A caddy is always grateful for, and solicitous of, suits of old tweeds. If you offer him a frock-coat, he suspects you of quizzing. The sumptuary laws in his set make the wearing of frock-coats or knickerbockers impossible. Nor is a gift of shirts appreciated by caddies. Our shirts are too light in colour for their fashion of wearing one till it is only fit to send to the papermaker.

On free greens the question of paying caddies is rather a troublesome one. There is usually an understood tariff. But as ragged children, miners out of work, discharged coachmen and butlers, drunkards who have spent their all, and ex-criminals are entitled to be paid on this scale for very inferior work, the professional carriers naturally expect more. What this more ought to be no man knows. It is useless to ask a friend what he pays, for he will not tell the truth. He will understate the amount. He dare not admit to having overpaid his caddy. Since John Stuart Mill and others made the law of supply and demand popular, the morality of stinginess, except where your name is to appear in a subscription list, has been fully admitted. Therefore to pay a caddy as much as will be accepted without grumbling, and to announce it, will lead you into an argument. Here is a specimen of the kind of thing I myself have gone through:-

'How much did you give your caddy?'

(Rather ashamed) 'Four shillings' (having given five).

'What nonsense! Three shillings are more than enough.'

'Perhaps' (rather mildly, but feeling right).

'Just spoiling the market. Three shillings for three hours' work! – more than any skilled workman can earn. Besides, it does no good – they just spend it.'

I submit; but alone in the evening I have it out with my hard-headed friend. I say:-

'Sir, when you accuse me of spoiling the market you are merely degrading free-trade principles to the position of handmaids of your selfish avarice. Free trade can live alongside of charity. If not, I go for charity. You seem to have heard of Adam Smith's *Wealth of Nations*, but not of his treatise on the *Moral Sentiments*. You have evidently read neither; or, if you will argue on the selfish principle, it is politic to overpay caddies. Cheapening golf is debasing golf. I wish it were compulsory to pay a sovereign a round. These school-boys and mechanics, and pot-hat golfers with a club and a cleek, are a nuisance. I wish gutta-percha balls had never been invented, and, as for eclipses, they are simple communism. They rob wealth of its advantages.

"The Caddies will only drink the more if over-paid," you say. Indeed! and to what good purpose do you apply the money you grudge to the poor? Is there something nobler in your gout and dyspepsia than in my caddy's red nose? Or no! I do not despise your gout (I feel a twitch myself), but your incapacity for taking pleasure in giving it (cheaply) to others is what I contemn. An Epicurean with the vices of a Stoic, and none of his virtues! I shall grossly overpay my caddy in future.'

On the newer greens, private ones, and those far from a town – in short, where it has been possible to reduce the carrying proletariat to subjection – the player will find a crowd of boys, with a sprinkling of meek men, near the club-house, from whom to choose a caddy. Under these circumstances a boy should be chosen. The men are no better than they, and, being grown up, not so scoldable. From boys, as I have said, the same standard of carrying cannot be expected as from professionals, but a well-chosen boy is satisfactory enough. He must not be too big. The big ones are usually louts who cannot stay the distance. He must not be too intelligent-looking. The bright-eyed, eager boy is apt to be admiring Nature whilst you are waiting for a club, and his interest in the game being awakened by a sharp word, it becomes for the moment too intense. He arranges the clubs whilst you are putting, or wanders into inconvenient situations to see you hole-out. The intelligent boy is sometimes himself a golfer. For the first half-round, whilst studying your game, he is a perfect treasure. After that, with the arrogance of youth, he assumes that he knows more than you do, and clubs are offered before asked, advice given in regard to distances, etc. Another kind of boy is chatty, and his anecdotes, autobiographical and local, which at first amuse, become intolerable as the match closes in darker and darker with each hole. An embryo village plumber or carpenter, neither clever nor stupid, will carry best.

On his home green the golfer soon settles upon a professional or a boy to his mind, according as his is a free or a controlled green. On the latter, when he is merely on a visit, there is not much trouble either. Any person has the moral courage to pay off a child at the end of the day if he does not suit, and to try another. It is different when you have once employed a man. Steaming, say to St. Andrews, the player is filled with anxious thought regarding caddies. He makes up his mind what manner of man to employ; but scarcely does he set foot in the station before he is bewildered by a dozen clamouring volunteers, unless he has had the forethought to disguise himself as a commercial traveller or as a tourist. Even disguise will only delay the inevitable for a few moments; when the tell-tale club box comes out of the van he is discovered. It is of course possible to flee before it is laid on the platform, leaving secret instructions with a trusty porter. But if the player has ever visited St. Andrews before, disguise and flight are of no avail. Years may have elapsed since his last visit; nevertheless he will be greeted by name. Several will assert that they carried for him before. He must either be more than humanly firm, or else be diplomatic, asserting, for instance, that he has a sprained wrist and does not intend to play, or before he has got to his lodgings he will find himself the thrall of perhaps the same being who poisoned his last visit. It might seem that the simplest course was to employ a boy so small that the weakest of men could dismiss him if unsatisfactory. But somehow there are none such at St. Andrews. There are carrying persons with the outward semblance of boys, but these chew, smoke and drink. It seems as if education or something bridged the space between childhood and manhood. Should the player escape to his lodgings unpledged, his best plan is to get down to the club as unobtrusively as possible, and make a selection from the window with an opera-glass. A caddy once engaged, most men make the best of him. Should he disappear for a day or two, having gone on the spree, you are not necessarily free from him. You have probably furnished the means for the debauch by paying some days' wages in advance, and it seems hard to sacrifice the money entirely, more especially as the miscreant will return humble and apologetic. Yet it is not so difficult as it seems, even for a man of average will, to dismiss a caddy who is not to his taste. The best plan is to pay him at the end of the day, and say nothing about it, making some excuse for taking your set into the club-house instead of leaving them in his charge. Next day you take on a fresh caddy by simply handing the clubs to him, and it is astonishing how little demur the old one will make. Caddies are a race as proud as they are improvident, and, however sycophantic under ordinary circumstances, they will take no other revenge for this insulting sort of dismissal than to assert that they left because underpaid, and because it is too wearisome to carry for such a bad golfer.

To summarise my advice in regard to caddies on greens to which the golfer is a temporary visitor, I advise him, where there is a corps of badged and licensed caddies, to choose the smallest boy who seems capable of getting round, and to keep him, if he stands still during play, and is generally within earshot when a club is required. It is necessary that he should not leave the ball in the hole, nor lose clubs on the way round. On free greens, persons having the outward semblance of boys are to be avoided, and a professional chosen if a good one be known to the player.

If, however, he is a complete stranger to the green, his safest course is to select a decrepit old man. His age proves him not to be an inconveniently excessive drinker, whilst being steady and still a carrier of clubs further proves that he is a meek, mild, mindless creature, who will trudge round without interfering.

PART TWO

Of Playing the Game

CHAPTER ONE

Of Driving in General

IT IS a common complaint that, with so many things to be thought of at golf, accuracy is almost impossible. This is not the way to state the case. It should rather stand: If points of style are thought about and trusted to, bad shots will be frequent. That there is some secret which, if discovered, would make our driving infallible is a belief which dies hard. Nostrum after nostrum is tried day after day. Hope is quickly followed by a despairing desire to break the whole set or spitefully to present them to a friend, so that he too may suffer. Time after time the golfer thinks he has discovered what he was doing wrong. He gushes about it, or gives half-a-crown to the professional who has found it out. Alas! there is no side road to golf. It can never be certain. With careful aiming for each shot, it may become pretty steady, but even with this there will be better and worse drives. It would be going too far to say dogmatically that nothing but aim must have a place in the golfer's thought, although it is perhaps best so; but certainly if stance, or swing, or address are dwelt upon it must be as subsidiary points. 'There is something wrong about my style,' says the golfer, 'which is causing me to drive so short.' 'Not at all,' say

35

Plate 1. Addressing for a Drive.

I, 'aim more accurately.' Hand and eye and body must concentrate themselves on, restrain themselves to, hitting cleanly, fairly, firmly; not greedily, wildly, gaily. The golfer cannot afford to allow a favourite muscle to disport itself. The eye is officer, the muscles liners, each doing the duty required of them and no more. The tongue only may wag as it will without doing harm or good.

There is no alternative. It is of no use to say to the ball, 'I will make thee magnificent gifts if thou wilt yield thy secret. I am ready to wrench and thump for thee, to stand nearer or further from thee, to bend the knee. I will imitate the swing of a Morris to conciliate thee.' The ball wants none of these self-glorifying gifts. Abandon body and will to hitting, and the hidden secret of the mystic $27\frac{1}{2}$ shall be revealed.

Still, the amateur golfer must be allowed to theorise to some extent. It is a necessary concession to him as a thinking animal. Within the indicated limits, it will do little or no harm; but because he does not think the professional is better than the amateur, the uncultivated beats the educated player. The former finds enough intellectual pabulum for his duller brain in the prosy principles of simply slogging. To grasp the idea of doing so, sufficiently occupies his thoughts. For an educated man to confine himself to so narrow a range is irksome. The professional's theorising does not go beyond 'I hit lazy – I heeled – I topped – I sclaffed – I toed.' To perceive so much is an effort of observation. The amateur must consciously exclude thought, if he is to confine himself to such elementary facts. It is noticeable that he (in distinction from the professional) asks, '*Why* did I heel – top – sclaff – toe?' – and if golf is to be a pleasure, not a business, he must be allowed to ask these things. The amateur, if keen, is inductive, deductive, inventive. If not, he is apt to give up the game as too simple. On the other hand, if he does not recognise 'hitting the ball' as his business, theory as his recreation, he becomes so bad a player that he nearly gives up.

'Keep your eye on the ball,' is the categorical imperative of the golfing world; below which there is room for much harmless digression. Say that I am playing very well, but that there is some irrational difference between my style with short spoon and driver. A professional would not know this of himself, or, if told, would not care. It is outside the range of his ideas. 'I'm driving fine,' he would say. But your amateur cannot rest till he has corrected one of the styles into uniformity with the other, or found a rational cause for the difference. If A. drives high, B. low, is it possible that A. with a university education, can rest satisfied with merely observing this fact? No. He will try to find out why, and, having done so, will either modify his style, or register to himself the conclusion that he prefers to drive high. The amateur ought to think. The man who buys a baffy because he can't drive with a cleek has not a cultivated mind. If he carry both – if his set is composed of a lot of preposterous inventions of his own, all of which he uses in turn, he increases the difficulties of the game indeed, but is nevertheless noble in not accepting defeat at the hands of any club. Experiment, so long as the major premise is not lost sight of, is the recreation which may be allowed to the golfer whilst attending to his business. It is a necessary concession to human nature; it is the spoonful of jelly with the Gregory's mixture; it is the working man's half-holiday, and a great many other analogous things. By all means let us have our clubs long or short, heavy or light, upright or flat. The golfer may be trusted in the long-run to give up anything which is too fanciful, although for a time he may spoil his play with a fad. It is harmless to buy clubs from professionals for gold, no better than what are for sale in the shops for four shillings.

The player may experiment about his swing, his grip, his stance. It is only when he begins asking his caddy's advice that he is getting on dangerous ground. A professional can play. It does not follow that he can teach others. He can comfortably assimilate foods and drinks (more particularly the latter) which would prostrate those he carries for on a bed of sickness. Is he therefore an authority on dietetics? But being constantly asked for advice, the professional has a few stock prescriptions which he gives recklessly, doing more harm than good. So anxious is the golfer to learn without plodding that he uses  these eagerly. The truth is, your caddy is a good judge of distance and direction. He

Figure 1.

can advise well what club to take, but as to how to use it, he may show, but ought not to be asked to advise. For instance, the player is persistently driving to the right or to the left of the line he wishes to follow. Let him correct his stand, but let him do so accepting the fact that he is standing wrong because his eye is at fault. Let him try to see straight. He ought to come away from his ball, and take up his position afresh with careful reference to his intended direction. But the usual thing is to accept the caddy's dictum (stand 'more behind' or stand 'more in front') blindly, and, without looking up, to scuffle about with the feet. When told, 'That will do,' the player either misses, being stiff and twisted; or – what is more common – he scuffles back to where he was at first, like a sitting hen moved from her eggs, and drives off the line. Having done this latter a dozen times, it seems that the position the caddy advises must be the solution of the difficulty. He, who has been driving persistently to the right has got into the position shown in diagram No. 1; in other words, his left foot has got nearer the ball than the right, which it has a strong natural inclination to do, and the tendency is to drive in the direction of the arrow, and not of the dots. What ought really to be done is that the player stand up naturally and aim

Figure 2.

carefully. The result of applying a correction such as 'stand behind' will not make the ball go straight until the awkward position of diagram No. 2 is reached.

It may seem that if the advice, instead of being, as it always is, 'Stand more behind,' were 'Change the position of one of your feet,' the result would not be to produce the style of Fig. 2. But this would alter the player's distance from the ball, and, instead of being the beginning of a cycle of fatal and deceptive good driving, would inaugurate a round of tops, heels, or pulls, to the immediate

Plate 2. Tom Morris Driving (1).

discredit of the caddy. If I wished to be cynical, I should say, therefore, 'Change one foot' is the better advice. But no! The proper thing to do is to try again. Anything else is absurd. Were a caddy to say, 'You would drive better with my arms,' or were he to offer the loan of any other limb, the nonsense would be evident. Yet the absurdity of using his eyes does not seem apparent. The player allows himself to be put in position like a lay figure. Even suppose he understands the orders, and does pose as the caddy intends, a lay figure cannot hit a ball. One man's mind cannot work another man's body.

The following is a specimen of what may be expected if a player hopes to drive by taking advice instead of aiming at the ball with his own eyes.

Player (1st shot). – 'Why did I heel that?'

Caddy. – 'Drawing in your arms.'

Player (2nd shot). – 'Why did I pull that?'

Caddy. – 'Drawing in your arms.'

Player (heeling again). – 'There! I did not draw in my arms that time.'

Caddy. – 'No, sir, ye cut it.'

Player (4th shot). – 'There's that confounded heel again.'

Caddy. – 'Ye didna cut it. Ye hit it clean enough that time; but ye were stanin' that way.'

Player (examining his club face after a vicious top). – 'Right off the heel too. What on earth is the meaning of it?'

Caddy. – 'Ye're fallin' in on the ball.'

Player (6th shot). – 'Another top.'

Plate 3. Tom Morris Driving (2). ('It's coming')

Caddy. – 'Ay, ye fell right back.'

Player. – 'Oh, hang it! With so many things to be thought of all at once, steady play is almost impossible.'

Having heard all that passed I here remark with a smile – meaning sardonic and oracular – 'Not almost, but quite impossible.'

Another error, nearly as bad as to take advice blindly, is for a player, when standing wrongly, to try to pull or push the ball according to the correction for direction desired. Let him rather correct his stance.

Faults covered by faults do not cancel each other. The second fault only gives the ball an additional chance of escape from the way it should go. Far the wisest course is to apply a direct remedy. The player whose driving is feeble should hit harder, unless it is because he is nipping, or not hitting off the middle of the club, in which cases he ought not to nip, or should aim for the centre of the head. It must be admitted, however, that it is much easier, for the moment, to apply indirect corrections, and few indeed are the formed golfers on whose style the cicatrices of early patchings are not visible. Some of these are almost harmless; but others may cripple the player permanently, although at the time, like new brooms, they sweep away the ball clean. For instance, there is a class of stereotyped faults whose origin is traceable to a miserable time when every ball was hopelessly heeled. If the wretched man (oh, how despondent he was then!) had only attributed his misery to the true cause – namely, that he was heeling – the fault would have corrected itself. But he found a royal road to the middle of his club. You see the former victims of heeling either standing nine

Plate 4. Tom Morris Driving (3).

feet from their ball and taking a header at it, or so crouching on their haunches that you are astonished, when the stroke is made, to find player and ball are not both left seated. If you see a golfer draw his club so slowly back that ten is easily counted before it begins to return, as a tyro he has been one of those who fervently wished that balls had no top. Again, there are men who face the east when they mean to go north. The sole ambition of these has been to drive a very long ball. They are victims to the truth that a ball so struck will sometimes go further north than one aimed to that part of the compass. But what does it profit when it as often goes east or west? Such fill men's gardens with golf-balls, and lose many more in the waves of the sea.

Do I maintain, then, the reader may ask, that everyone ought to have the same style? By no means; on the contrary, for you or me to model ourselves on a champion is about as profitless as to copy out *Hamlet* in the hope of becoming Shakespeare. If we have a neat style, so be it; and if we began before our hair was grey or gone, it probably so is. But for a fat man to model himself on a swank youth is frivolous. We cannot ignore our deformities. Our shoulders are heavy, our fore-arm puny; it is useless to rebel. A very easy long swing is impossible with such a configuration. We may play well – beat the swank youth very likely, – but only if we are content with a stiff style. Are we lank and loose-limbed? – So will our driving be, if left to develop naturally.

On the other hand, there is no more fruitful source of bad golf than to suppose that there is some best style for each individual which must be searched out by him if he is to get the best results out of himself. In a broad and general way, each player ought to have, and has, a style which is the reflection of himself – his build, his mind, the age at which he began, and his previous habits. The ex-cricketer reflects cricket. The rowing-man has a straight back, and there are characteristics in each golfer the history of which it is more or less difficult to trace. This is his style; and however much he may feel he modifies it, to an onlooker it will remain the same – because it is the same. It is not the general principles that a man has before him (of these he is seldom conscious) when trying to find out his absolute best. It is some minor detail of which he exaggerates the importance – some particular twitch, which has arrested his attention after a very satisfactory drive. This will be stubbornly pursued till it is exaggerated into a mannerism to which it is secretly believed everything good in his driving is due. If golfers could only become convinced that no mannerism is of the slightest value, that there are fifty different styles (by style I mean here the petty variables of which alone we are conscious) in which a good shot can be made, that it is not indispensable to repeat in the next the same movements felt in one good shot, bad ones would be less frequent. There is, I repeat, a categorical imperative in golf – 'Hit the ball;' but there are no minor absolutes. There is no best shape, or weight, or lie of clubs – no best stance, grip, or swing. From the nature of the case, one does not change his driver during the round; but the other things may vary every shot – nay, will, unless one makes a point of preventing them, sacrificing ease and accuracy to a consistency which, if stubbornly insisted on, may permanently cramp driving. There is no better proof of this argument than to watch a boy of about twelve, who hits every ball clean and (for his strength) far, of whom there are very many. At this age even the broad features of style are unsettled. At one moment he swings round his neck, at the next round his shoulder, his feet near together or wide apart, according to the unconscious fancy of the moment. And yet each ball flies away with unerring certainty. This should teach us that when we think we see what we are doing wrong, or what we are doing right, that when we cling to this bit of style or avoid that, we are merely distracting our attention from the main issue.

CHAPTER TWO

Of Style in Driving

For the purpose of analysis the swing of the golfer may be divided into three parts: 1st, Position; 2nd, Address; 3rd, Swing proper.

Position. – Some treatises on the game tell us in feet and inches the distance the player ought to stand from the ball; in degrees, the angle at which it ought to be placed between his feet. Such information, whether true or not, is unpractical. Arithmetic is required to count the shots, but cannot assist us in making them; and as for mensuration – well! A six-inch scale marked on the putter shaft often prevents disputes. Roughly speaking, however, it may be laid down that one ought to stand what professionals call square to the ball – that is to say, facing at right angles to the direction it is meant to drive in. Any decided deviation from this position is a mistake, although scarcely anyone adheres to it absolutely. Many place the left foot nearer the ball than the right, commonly called standing 'in front' (though different from the fault

Figure 3.

Standing 'in front'.

of doing so illustrated in Fig. 1, p. 39), and lean more weight on the former than on the latter. This is because the left leg of most men is the stronger. Some of the finest players stand to their ball in this way; but on the whole it is to be avoided, because it tends to produce wildness and uncertainty of driving. Obviously the position offers facilities for a long swing back, and those who are lured on by the charms of an occasional raker will adopt it. Why occasional? The reason seems to be that when the heel of the left foot leaves the ground most of the weight of the body is supported on its toes, which unsteadies the player's balance, and consequently his driving. The remedy is scarcely to let the heel leave the ground at all – a correction made by all steady drivers who have acquired this style. The segment of swing thus chopped off is, however, lost entirely. It cannot be added to the other end, as, of course, the stance which takes the right shoulder out of the road brings the other more forward. The result is shorter driving if

Figure 4.
Standing 'square'.

steady off the tee, but not from bad lies; for this stance, by enabling the player to get 'his shoulders well into it,' is very commanding. On the whole, however, it is better to stand square or open as in Figs. 4 or 5. This gives freer scope for a full second half to the swing, which, I shall insist further on, is of more importance than the first half. Exaggeration, even conscious posing, in either direction, will produce, in the first case, pulling, wildness, topping; in the second, heeling, skying, or at best feebleness.

If we observe a player who stands 'square' about to strike, it will be apparent that his ball is at a more obtuse angle to his left than to his right foot. If the player stands 'in front' (Fig. 3), as it is called, the ball is more nearly still in a line with the left, the opposite being true when the stance is 'open.' But in practice he ought not to attempt to measure this angle, for the all-sufficient reason that his measurement will be wrong. To prove this, we have but to ask an experienced player who stands 'square,' at what angle he poses to his ball. He will say at an equal angle from each foot. We have but to watch him play to be convinced that he is mistaken. That he cannot measure it will be made evident by a

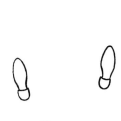

Figure 5.

Standing 'open'.

little experiment regarding another point. Some players turn their toes in, some out. (Which is right? Either, provided the position be not strained.) Now, if you place yourself opposite a ball, at what some books call the proper angle, it will be found that by pivoting on the heels, although your place, or its, is in no way changed, a drive would be impossible without lifting one foot and putting it down somewhere else.

As the angle at which the player ought to stand can only be determined by instinct, as a comprehensive glance at feet and ball will give no information even to engineers accustomed to mensuration, so there is no measureable proper distance at which we ought to be from the ball. Much depends on the lie of the club, its length, that of the man, and his style. Yet the varying of it is a common cause of bad driving. Quite suddenly, from unconsciously changing it, a player goes off his game: without knowing it, he begins to hold his hands too far reached out, or to stoop forward with his body. It is useless for him to note his proper distance some time when he is driving well, for he may maintain that and yet be all wrong. For instance, he may be cancelling his overreach by standing very upright, or stooping and tucking in his arms. Always to take a natural pose towards the ball must be the result of habit. Even the best players go wrong occasionally from getting into the way of standing at the wrong distance. The worst of it is, stooping or overreaching soon feels natural, and the bad driving is ascribed to some other cause. In its proper place, I will point out a few of the results as regards the ball, which ought to awaken suspicion that our position has got wrong.

How far apart the feet ought to be is the next point. About this, as about so many other things, there is no hard and fast rule. It is sufficient to point out that the closer they are, the freer will be your swing; but when they get too near together your driving will become feeble and uncertain in direction. On the other hand, a wide stride stiffens the player, thus shortening his driving, although it gives him power. In a bunker, or in a bad lie, it is politic to straddle more than usual, if you remember at the same time to swing short.

Address. – After taking their stance, most players are in the habit of making some preliminary motions with their club before proceeding to drive. In some cases these flourishes are slight, in others more free: but, whichever they be, they are only reasonable and advantageous if made to waken up the muscles and to let the hands settle to their grip. With too many players, addressing the ball is merely an excuse for other thoughts. One will take this opportunity to scuffle round his ball, another to get nearer it or further from it, another to lift his toes and assure himself that his heels are well on the ground, another to look at his feet or the position of his hands, another to hunch up a shoulder, another to turn in a toe. In other words, the time during which the player should be getting concentrated on the work of hitting, many waste in thinking of the quackeries which they hope will take the responsibility of aiming off their shoulders. Some of those who thus waste the precious moments make no pretence of shaking themselves together. They stand stock-still. What are they thinking of? Are they bidding a fond adieu to the ball, shrewdly suspecting that the club head may not be passing that way on its return journey. Slowly and reluctantly at last club and ball part, when suddenly whack! From others there are storm warnings. The club rises, and returns solemnly – Once! Twice! Thrice! The player seems to say, 'I warn you, look out. Look out once! Twice! Thrice! Very well, take that, and off you go!' Then there is the elbow twitch, which seems to say, 'I am just shaking my clothes loose to go for you, and getting my arms free to follow you.' It is a bragging kind of address, which threatens a strong blow and is really preliminary to a weak one. The confident twiddle which makes no pretence of aiming, but commandingly points out to the ball the direction of the hole, and is followed by an angry quick swing, such as comes unawares behind a disobedient child, is not so sure to strike home as the blow it is compared to.

Some twiddles are complementary to faults which the player proposes to avoid. A long, slow straight motion over the ball foreshadows a determination to follow it well. A stiff small one means that the player is bent on gripping tight. A quick jerky one betrays the intention of driving a screamer. There is the sanguine, the phlegmatic, the healthy, the headachy flourish, and a thousand more. None of these, except in so far as they suggest that the player has a right or a wrong idea as to how the fact of a palpable hit is to be accomplished, are essential. But placing the club behind the ball for an instant after them is essential, if the shot is not to be more or less bad. Although the address is usually a shadow of things to come, it is no guarantee of them. Free preliminaries are quite compatible with a cramped performance, and *vice versa*... It may be said, then, why not abandon them altogether? Why not place the club behind the ball, and strike at once? In these cases, where addressing the ball consists in merely making ornamental flourishes, or when they are gone through to give the player time to speculate on the chances of a miss, or to call up before his imagination a view of the bunker in front which he has just taken a last glance at, they would be better dispensed with. But, properly apprehended, they have their uses, some of which we have indicated: the chief one, I wish now to insist upon.

'How ought I to grip my club?' is a question which causes lifelong trouble to, and bars the progress of, many players. Addressing the ball means working their hands into some cramped position. They arrange the left hand tight, the right loose or tight, in the palm or in the fingers, under the club, over it, or with the knuckles pointing in some prescribed direction, according to whose disciple they are. There is scarcely a modification of holding with two hands which someone has not adopted as his grip, each giving its owner a sense of command over the club, so long as it is at rest, behind the ball. That a player should give attention to this important matter is right enough; but the mistake usually made is to get the hands into the most efficient position for dealing a heavy, instead of a swift blow, without reference to the most essential point in a grip – namely, that it be so arranged as to prevent the club either slipping or twisting in the palms during any part of the swing. If a player gets his hands under the club-handle (see Figs. 8 and 9) it is impossible to take more than a half swing without letting go. If (see Fig.10) he have the right more under than the left, and tight (a grip one is apt to adopt when a 'screamer' is contemplated), anything but a swing round the waist must bring the club-head back to the ball turned in (which is the secret of the screamer when it comes off, and also the cause of its failing so often).

If anyone by chance has read this last paragraph carefully, he will feel pretty certain that I am about to describe the proper position and tightness of each hand. But he will be wrong. On the contrary, my view is that players may take great liberties with their grip, – at least with that of their right hand – without affecting driving. The club may be sunk in the palm, to save a sore finger, or held in the fingers if the palm be painfully horny, without prejudice to play, so long as it is so held as not to slip or turn one hair's-breadth throughout the shot. Nay! In the right it may be even allowed to turn. In fact, if a player grip as in Fig. 10, he must hold loose with the right, and allow the club to slip round if his swing be perfect, otherwise his wrist becomes locked. Of this a trial swing will convince anyone. It is only possible with a grip as in Figs. 6 and 7 for the right hand to remain glued to the club throughout a perfect swing. 'How is the grip to be tested for adherence during the swing?' is the real question, which the address ought to solve thus: – Having placed himself opposite the ball, let the player take

Figure 6. Proper grip, hands 'over' or 'above'.

hold of his club loosely, but so that, if held short, the end of the shaft would pass under the wrist bones (somewhat as in Figs. 6 and 7). Let him swing it backwards and forwards freely over the ball, describing an elongated eight, whose length is limited by the locking-point of the wrist joints. After two or three such continuous figures have been described, the hands, still holding loosely, will settle themselves into a proper relation to each other, and to

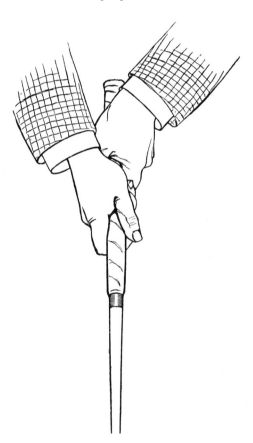

Figure 7. Proper grip, hands 'over' or 'above'.

the shot. The club will then be placed behind the ball, the grasp tightened just as it is, and the blow delivered. Whether both should be tightened, or only the left – whether it is into the fingers, or the palm, these movements are to adjust the club – are immaterial points, which may be left to individual taste. Nor ought the amount of tightening to be treated as important. Some only tighten a little, some as much as they can; all that can be said is, that the limit of permissible looseness is overstepped when, in the course of sweeping away the ball, there is any slipping or turning in the left hand at the very least. The preliminary flourish under discussion will be detected in the driving of the best and freest players. Should an elongated eight be found on any ancient Egyptian monument, it is certainly the symbol for golf, and will prove that venerable nation to have played the game. I say this flourish can be 'detected' in a good style; but a practised player does not require to pass over his ball more than once, or he may even pretermit all, except the merest rudiment. He has a proper hold at once, without searching for it, and can at once proceed unhesitatingly to strike. There is no pause, after the club has been placed behind the ball, to allow a final and fatal alteration to be made.

It is interesting confirmation of the soundness of what I am advancing, that fine players, many of whom are proverbial for the instantaneousness of their address, are often more elaborate in a big match. Whereas a mere rudiment of a flourish is all they ordinarily indulge in, this becomes one or more complete eights, when a single mistake might be fatal. It is as if they said, 'I am almost certain to grip rightly; but it is as well to test it.'

Plate 5. Jim Morris Driving (1).

Whether this plan of preliminary flourish is or is not the best, there is no doubt the grip should be found by some sort of trial swing, not by placing the club behind the ball, and settling down as comfortably as possible. The true grip is that which accommodates itself to a free swing, not to a commanding stance. Indeed players may be divided into two classes, according as they act upon or ignore this principle. The one arrives at the position of the hands typified in Figs. 6 and 7, and perhaps Fig. 10; the other is prone to the fault shown in Figs. 8 and 9. The one makes its flourishes, places its club for an instant behind the ball, and without hesitation strikes. If they allow it to dwell longer, it is not comfortable perhaps. Nor need it be. Ease whilst swinging, not whilst at rest, is the essential thing. The other finds its grip whilst the club is at rest, and then proceeds to flourish. Take the case of a player of this class who makes the orthodox figure-eight gyration. He takes his grip, makes a motion over the ball, and, unless by chance it is a true one, disturbs it by so doing. You may see him pause a moment to rearrange it; the other accepts the disturbance as a proper correction. Whatever the prowess of the player, his class in this respect can be detected by watching whether, after putting his club finally behind the ball, he hesitates or strikes at once. Nearly all bad players belong to the class which does not arrive at its grip by experiment but dogmatically; not that all in it are bad, however. Their grip may by chance be good, or they may have the tact to accommodate their swing to the conditions they have imposed upon it. But assuredly this common error of taking hold of the club in the most comfortable way for aiming at the ball,

Plate 6. Jim Morris Driving (2).

rather than for the blow, has to answer for many monstrous styles, efficient and otherwise.

Swing. – 'My swing' is a constant theme for conversation with the young golfer. He is forever making it quicker or slower, longer or shorter, some skilful player being in his mind's eye, whom he fancies he is imitating – or rather, whom he is imitating in every way except one – the only one which will give him a true style – not thinking about it when playing, which the good player never does. His one problem is to sweep the ball away with speed. This is done by his body remaining a firm fulcrum for the lever composed of his arms and club. His swing back ends when the contact of his left biceps with his chest prevents it going further, his wrists remaining as taut as he can keep them. Not that he thinks of this, or of anything but sweeping the ball away. Let the beginner devote himself to the same problem. For a long time he will have a short swing; but it will lengthen quickly enough. There is not the slightest danger of its not doing so, unless he fall into the error of supposing that the more gently he hits the surer he is.

Many begin in quite another way. They see the professional's club swishing round his back, and they determine, at all costs, to get theirs as far round. By a variety of schemes they accomplish this, and become the proud possessors of a concatenation of contortions, in which no one but themselves recognises the resemblance to a full swing. Some swing naturally to a certain point, then, letting their wrists bend, drop the thing down their backs, draw it up again, and proceed to drive the ball. In the meantime their position has almost certainly changed in some way, so that the club head does not return to the ball along the same imaginary line it went from it. Others avoid the natural check of the biceps against the body by sticking out the left elbow and passing the arm round the neck, which, being thinner, allows the hands to get as far as the back of the head. To play in this way it is usual, or at least better (if I may be allowed to use an approbatory adjective at all in reference to such a matter), to employ upright clubs, although they will not overcome the inevitable uncertainty of direction. To get the club to the back of the neck, it must be drawn away at a tangent to the direction the ball is to be driven in. To prevent it going to the left, the player has to resort to some counter modification. He must, after impact, let his arms away to the right. Should he be lucky enough to catch the ball at the exact instant when his curve is practically parallel to the direction it is meant to go in, although 'cut' the shot will be straight; if he reaches it a hair earlier, it will be 'pulled' – a hair later, it will be 'heeled.' These are the terms the player would use. It would be more exact to describe the three drives as a cut to the right, a cut to the left, and a straight cut. Some who drive in this way stand well in front of the ball, and thus reduce their curve more nearly to a straight line; but I have seen one get rid of the cut entirely, which they might do by turning their back altogether to the line of fire.

The left elbow joint, as a joint, has no part in a true swing. But it is a prevalent habit to close it a little after the club has circled back as far as it naturally should. This is not quite so silly a way of giving oneself the sensation of swinging far as is dropping the club over the shoulder by means of the wrist joints. But it is foolish enough, particularly if the player begins his swing with straight instead of slightly bent arms, in order to have more elbow-bending to do afterwards. Anyone can see, when it is pointed out, that this joint work is merely a break which has to be mended before the sweep forward commences. Yet good players often take to it for a time if their driving is not satisfactory, feeling, in spite of common sense, that they are lengthening their reach.

It would be profitless to describe more of the endless twists and twiddles with wrists and elbows which golfers acquire, seeking for a long swing in the wrong way, which is the same thing as seeking for it at all. Hundreds of balls are daily 'foozled' which would be struck but for these little spasms after the club has reached its proper goal. One sees them all over the links. They remind us sometimes of hairs which have grown too long and split at the ends; sometimes they suggest blind men groping their way.

It must strike anyone who thinks of it as curious that so many should wander so far from the main road in search of a swing. One reason is, as already indicated, that swings are among the things which, according to Longfellow, 'are not what they seem.' Hence the errors of imitators. The professional appears to wind his club round his back. It is not so. It is the club which winds round him, not because he wishes it to do so, but because his muscles, though knit, have their natural elasticity. The player is in the centre of a circle, at a point in the circumference of which is the ball. The more nearly his club head describes a perfect segment whilst driving, the better. But it is not possible to make a true circle swiftly with a springy wire, which the player is, or a springy club shaft, if you will. He is even a bad shaft, weak in some places – for example, at the wrist. Let a player look upon his left arm as a part of a club. He can see at once that it will not lengthen his driving to have a break in it somewhere. He might as well expect to lengthen his swing by putting joints in the actual wooden shaft, strengthened (say) with strong India-rubber bands, spliced over them, to imitate human joints. In other words, every joint of the fine driver's left arm below the shoulder is as taut as the extensor muscles (I rather think these are the ones) keep it without undue attention to the point. I have said the left arm. I should say nothing about the right, were it not that I might be supposed to mean that it too was to be treated as part of the shaft, and that I was advocating that stiff dunch from the shoulder with arms not naturally bent but rigidly straight, by which many late beginners remove their ball from the tee. In true driving, the left arm has to accommodate itself in the swing back. It is loose and obedient. Its elbow joint has to flex, and it is not until it is brought back to within a foot of the ball that it joins with the other in the work of driving – not till after impact that it becomes master, the other slave.

Fine players are not only apt to lead others astray by appearing, to the superficial observer, loose and flexible in every joint, but knotless contortionists, who are really so, look stiff and ponderous. Learners are thus doubly impressed with the idea that a free and a flabby swing are one and the same thing. Nor is it easy for them to be disabused of their error. No man can see himself strike, and thus learn that the swing he has adopted, the flexibility he feels, is visible not as ease but as awkwardness. Nor is there much chance of finding out his errors by comparing his sensations with those of good players, who, as a rule, pay no attention to such matters. Curiously enough, if pressed to say something, it will often be (I have got this answer from many professionals), 'My longest balls are when I feel I've got my wrists into it.' This misleads the tyro terribly, although it is true. The professional gets this sensation from a full, taut, India-rubbery swing. It is the result of his determination to get back to the ball as soon as possible. The other takes it to mean that he ought to get as far from it as he can by allowing the club to master his wrist. One day an adversary sought my praise for the way in which he was driving with his iron. I said (which was apparent), 'You have a fuller swing with it than with the play club.' 'You mean the opposite,' he answered. I repeated my commentary, and he rejoined, 'That is curious, I've been off my iron play, and am getting into it again by taking a half swing.' But I was right, which he admitted after experimenting in the matter. In driving from the tee this player had a long – a very long – swing, if by that is meant the distance the club head meandered away from the ball before coming back to it. In addressing, his arms, instead of having the natural bend, were straight as bars. They took the club a long way off, flexion of the left elbow took it further, flexion of the wrists another foot. By stretching, over-reaching, relaxing, his journey was the longest possible; but travelling far and swinging long are different matters. With his iron he described a true segment of a circle, every muscle as stiff and taut all the time as when the ball was struck.

In short, then, a good swing seems to the onlooker swift and flexible; but if the player feels supple, he exhibits an awkward, stiff, straggling movement. The player ought to be, in his own hands, a stiff bow which he bends and shoots with. Of course, by practice, he learns to bend this bow with ease, and to shoot with accuracy. But when he goes off his driving the remedy is not to lengthen and loosen the string, but rather to tighten and shorten it.

Hitherto I have spoken chiefly of errors in swinging developed in the region between the shoulders and the point of the club. Those that can be made with the rest of the body are of a simpler nature, because, in regard to them, swings for the most part are what they seem. It is without dispute that the shoulder joints are to be used with perfect freedom and flexibility. If a man is reaching too far with them he does not need to be told. He feels his neck sink into his body. He knows that the more freely his trunk oscillates on its supports, the better. He knows that, his position once taken, his body ought not to sway to the right not to the left, forward nor backward. Not that he can count upon its never doing so. We often get into tricks of falling backwards, swaying away to the right, etc., but we are conscious of them. Everyone knows that whether he plays with straight or bent knees, they must remain straight or bent throughout the shot. The necessity for standing firm on the feet, however, although admitted, is not universally appreciated. There is a prevalent disposition to plant them so as to make sure that the left heel will come away from the ground, as if this were of as much importance as a firm foundation. Indeed, I am inclined to think that it is of none at all. That the heel of

Plate 7. Sayers Driving (1)

good players does come away from the ground, there is no doubt; but, in the case of many of the very best, how reluctantly! – and merely as if torn from it by the force of the swing. As I have said before, most fine players (I might say all who began young) have no theory, and can give but scant advice. One of the very best, when pressed for answer as to a certain peculiarity in his stance, said, 'Do I stand so? I didn't know (said as if it meant, 'I don't care'). The only thing to think about is planting your feet in the ground – it doesn't matter where, so long as they are glued down.' I said, ' But your heel leaves the ground when you swing.' 'Does it? Are you sure? I don't think so.'

A chapter on *Swing* would be incomplete without some reference to the maxim 'Slow back.' Everyone acknowledges and feels that it is a sound one; but many fail to put it in practice, particularly those who have a slow, ponderous style. This seems to be a contradiction in terms, but it is true nevertheless. The fact is, 'slow back' is not an accurate term for what is meant. Those learning the game get puzzled. The professional does not appear to practise what he preaches. He seems to swing, and does swing, swiftly. What is really demanded by 'slow back' is not absolute but relative slowness. If we compare the true swing to an India-rubber band, 'slow back' means that it is to be stretched more slowly than it will recoil. By practice, men learn to set the spring quickly, and the rate is of no importance provided there be nothing approaching to a jerk or wrench back. You must not be able to hear the club swish through the air as on the return journey. 'Stiff back,' 'taut back,' or 'sway back,' would be a more explicit phrase. Whatever

Plate 8. Sayers Driving (2)

it be called, the thing itself is a *sine qua non* of fine driving. When a player is merely pushing his hands round his neck instead of swinging, however slowly, and twitching them forward again, his caddy will be tempted to tell him he is too quick back, as much as if he is jerking it up round his shoulder. A good player who has temporarily fallen into any form of (to invent an ugly word) unpendulumness, on being warned that he is too quick back, will understand that he is not tightening all the muscles properly used in swinging equally – that he is merely flopping at the ball with his arms. A bad player, who has never learned what a true swing is, may only be made worse with 'slow back.' It may induce him to lift the club up softly and gingerly, with the kind of slowness necessary to grab a fly on his right ear, but which has nothing to do with driving a ball. A true swing is not like flashing a sword through the air, but as if forcing it through a strongly resisting medium.

Whilst the minds of golfers are, for the most part, unduly exercised about their swing before impact, tricks, jerks, and false curves in the other segment of their circle are scarcely thought about or observed. We wonder that A., with a short, spasmodic twiddle, should drive further and more steadily than B., who gets credit for quite a professional style. But if we look (not a natural thing to do, because the eyes instinctively wink when club and ball click together), B. will be seen 'to follow,' whilst A. pulls up short. Of the two evils, crampedness after striking is perhaps more fatal than before it, or rather it would be more accurate to say that no one is contented to swing short back as many habitually do forward.

It is unnecessary to enlarge upon this part of the swing. What has been already said applies equally to both halves of it. The second part ought to be, as far as possible, a reflection of the first. In the case of good players who stand square to the ball, it is so in every respect, being a little shorter or longer proportionately according as a man stands 'in front' or 'open.' Falling in, falling back, etc., are as apt to occur in one half as in the other. Swaying the whole body forward after the ball is as likely to cripple driving as swaying away from it when taking the club back. It is not so common to let the right heel leave the ground too much at the end of a stroke, as it is to rise too much on the left toe. Nor do men need to keep a tight hold of themselves lest the club wander away by itself in search of a long swing. Loose-jointedness here rather betrays itself by a check a foot past the tee and a finishing twitch with the wrists.

CHAPTER THREE

Advice to Beginners

THE BEGINNER who has read the foregoing chapters will be apt to re-read the first sentence, and to agree with those who complain that accuracy is almost impossible with so many things to remember; or, if he sees that it is not intended he should think of them all, he will still be puzzled to understand which are the elementary, which the more advanced, instructions. Accordingly I propose in this chapter (even at the risk of some repetition) to write a little sermon for the young player.

Let the beginner shake himself down naturally before the ball, and hit. Till he has done this for a good many days, no advice has either use or meaning. During this first stage it is probable that he will be quite delighted with his driving, and with good reason. His attention being entirely directed to hitting – his curiosity about how to hit not being so far aroused – he makes good shots. In many respects a man naturally attacks the ball in the proper way. He stands up, stands firm, does not force; and although his swing is of course stiff, it is not artificial. From the very first some players, however, make the mistake of treating the ball as a heavy object, whilst in reality it has, for practical purposes, no weight, and ought to be swept away, not jerked. In a bunker or a hard hole it becomes heavy, and nothing will do but a jerk; but from the turf the problem is to shave it cleanly off. Again, early cricket, and many other games with balls, start most beginners on their golfing career with a wrong grip. The handle of the club is opposite the third waistcoat button instead of being as low as the length of the arms naturally let it go. They wish to drive as much in cricket form

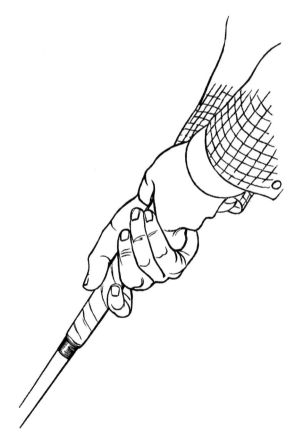

Figure 8. Hands too far 'round', or 'under'.

74

as the shape of the club will allow. Not that anyone thinks of liter-
ally golfing with a straight bat. They are freed from that restraint,
and enjoy swiping across the wicket. But this cannot be allowed. A
bad cricketing style is not a good golfing one. The beginner must
learn that golf is the very opposite of cricket, that he must get his
hands as much down at it as up at the other. He must use his club
like a scythe; must sweep, not strike the ball. In my opinion the

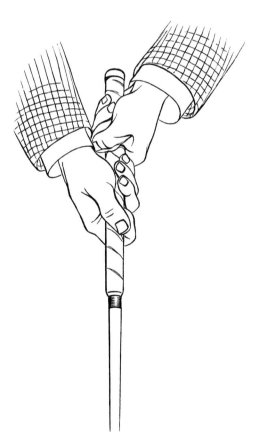

Figure 9. Hands far too 'round', or 'under'.

75

extent to which the player gets his hands over the club cannot be exaggerated. To have them well over is a *sine qua non* of an easy style. Beginners and others do not like the position until they have proved it, until patience and experience convince them that the grip which is most convenient for catching the ball a hammer-like thud is not the best either for far or sure.

I say, 'until they have proved it.' Lucky for them, if they ever do. A very large percentage of players live and play and die with their knuckles pointing too much towards the ground, with their club at too obtuse an angle with their arms, and consequently without the possibility of ever having a perfect swing (Figs. 8 and 9). Seen from the front, a perfect player's arms and club appear at the angle to each other shown in Fig. 6.

Imperfection lies between that and a straight line from shoulder to club head. Why getting the knuckles too far round is so common, so almost universal (see Figs. 8 and 9), is (besides that it gives the hammering power already referred to) that it prevents the wrists being used, and leads quickly to fairly steady driving, whilst the true position enables them to be employed, with consequent feeble and uncertain hitting. I would therefore strongly impress upon beginners the advisability of having their hands well over the club – of becoming steady by keeping their wrists taut, rather than by so gripping the club that their joints cannot bend. I say 'hands.' It should rather be 'hand' – the left hand. The right will look after itself. If the tyro acquires a grip which prevents him seeing his left knuckles, and which shows him instead more than the first joints of his fingers (compare Figs. 7 and 9), if his club handle point to his waistcoat instead of well below that garment, there is no reason why he should not become an effective, but he never will be a pretty, driver – a true, full style of the orthodox sort is impossible. The fault must be compensated by either a short, a broken, an overhead swing, or by some other modification, pronounced or slight in proportion to the cause. Let anyone grip in this way, swing a club back to his shoulder, examine the constrained position of his right wrist, and he will see that one of these things is inevitable.

If he acquire a grip as in Fig. 10, it would be hypercritical to interfere. As I have said, great latitude may be allowed to the right hand in this matter, particularly if it grasp loosely. But should anyone be so misguided as to hold disproportionately in the opposite way – that is, with the right hand over and the left under – farewell to all chance of even passable driving.

It is not generally till after the first week that the golfer begins to think about his game – to wish to know how it is done, in order that he may improve. With these inquiries his troubles begin, and let us hope that, with patience and common sense, he will get through them without crippling his style.

He will soon hear on all sides, 'Keep your eye on the ball.' Of course one must see the thing which is to be struck; but it is a mistake to insist upon it as if it were very difficult. If the beginner glares at the ball too determinedly it will mesmerise him, so that the hammering will be a distraction, and cuts from former tops appear to be fatuous mouths smiling derisively.

Then it comes to be a question with the beginner whether he

ought to go in for a full or for a half swing. If he must have an answer – if he must have a name for, and an ideal on which to mould, his blow, let it be a half swing. It will be some time before his unpretending thump can be classed at all; but no matter. It ought to be more like a half swing than anything else; it will grow into that, and from that into a full one, unconsciously, as the fetters of awkwardness fall from his limbs; but if he try for a full swing at once, he will not get it – he will merely acquire the habit (difficult to correct later on) of allowing his club to wander aimlessly about his back and shoulders.

In the laudable endeavour to drive far (and no man should ever accept the position of a weak player), the beginner has to stumble through many errors before mastering the secret of where and how to apply his force. There is one the beginner is certain to fall into. In order to get a good sweep at the ball, instead of causing his trunk to revolve on its own axis, he sways it back over his right leg. One feels as if tremendous force were acquired in this way. So there is, but of the wrong sort – slow, ponderous, clumsy. Even a ball clean hit, and getting the full result of this swaying motion, does not go far. But it seldom is hit, and no more wonder than that it should be missed if struck at whilst the player is walking. Swaying thus is a standing walk, a term which may be objected to, although it ought to be as intelligible as the accepted phrase, a 'standing jump.' It is perhaps as well to advise young golfers to have both hands close together; at all events, it is but fair to warn them that every inch which separates them takes ten yards off the length of their shot.

These few hints are ample theoretical equipment for many months. But the beginner will get many more, to which I advise him to turn a deaf ear. Every old hand will be anxious to persuade him that his own last crotchet is the one thing needful. He will be told that the great point is to keep his hands tight, or not to keep them tight, or one slack, his elbow in, or his elbow out, to let the club follow the ball, or his arms follow the ball, etc. etc. Naturally he thinks these people know. He tries one and all, getting as confused as if he were selecting a new religion. The fact is, there are more bad teachers than good, and if the beginner must have advice, let him consult a really first-class player, who will probably tell him he knows nothing about grips, or elbows, or following, and that all he has to do is stand firm and smite hard.

If the beginner is liable to be confused by his friends, the danger is much greater from his caddy. The former only give advice when it is asked, the latter volunteers it, and insists. There are such things as good professional coaches. On the whole, it is better not to allow your caddy to interfere. Most of them advise a thousand and one things within the hour. They feed babes with strong meat, and expect to, or at least try to, make them full-grown golfers within an hour. Besides things good enough in themselves if they could be digested, two pieces of advice which they mostly insist upon are positive poison. One, already spoken of in the last chapter, is that the player should rise upon his left toe. The swing not yet being so full and free as to tear the heel from the ground, by acting on this advice the beginner is simply left with a few spare inches of leg which he does not know what to do with. He may double them under him out of the road, but most likely he will use them to sway his body away back over the right leg, his caddy thus actually encouraging him to commit this common and fatal mistake of beginners. The other is insisting on the right thumb being over, not on, the club. If (which is likely enough, as we have seen) the beginner is holding his club as uprightly as possible, both hands too much under the club, it is absolutely impossible for him

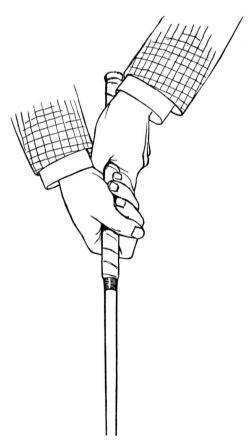

Figure 10. Unequal grip, right hand 'under'.

to strike at all if he obeys. His grip well over, he may do it; but ought not to unless it is natural – perhaps not even then, as at this early stage it foreshadows an intention of driving with the wrists, and opens the way to these wanderings of the club round the back – these so called long swings of which I have already said a good deal.

Leave the thumb where it is. By degrees, if the player allows himself to acquire his art without prejudice, it will slip into its proper place, getting out of the way to allow a fuller swing. But at first it is needed to guide the stroke, and if not allowed to be used, the beginner will effect his purpose by some other means, perhaps burying his club in his palm so as to work with the end of the second joint instead of with the point of the thumb. This inevitably 'turns in the nose' of the club, and it breaks. His faith in his caddy costs many a beginner much money and many sad rounds, in which his set gets reduced to some irons and some headless shafts. It is lucky for his golf if in the end he rebels against the oracle. If he does not, his grip with the right hand is a difficulty ever after. It remains twisted, and to do any work at all, the body and legs have to twist too.

For some time the beginner (I am speaking of men, not boys) makes marked and regular progress, until suddenly one day there is a breakdown, which crushes his sanguine hope that his march towards perfection was to be smooth and rapid. It is the first of many which will occur from time to time so long as he is able to hold a club. To avoid them altogether is impossible, but their number may be lessened, their severity checked, by wisdom and care. When the beginner is getting on swimmingly, let him not be carelessly confident, for pride goes before a fall. Nor when his driving is very satisfactory ought he to attempt to note what he is doing, so as to be able to return to it if a relapse occurs. This in itself is the beginning of backsliding. Golf refuses to be preserved like dead meat in tins. It is living, human and free, ready to fly away at the least sign of an attempt to catch and cage it. It will confute your logic if you, as it were, stand aside and try to produce it by causes. With patient attention to hitting, not relaxed even when we are in the full pride of good play, our relapses will be fewer and less severe; but there is no means by which we can secure uniform progress. In proportion as the wave of advance is great, so will be the back draught. Let not the learner be discouraged by it, and begin to doubt lest the tide has turned. Golfers often speak of their game. The best the learner has ever played is his game, even supposing it is a third better than what he has relapsed to. It will come again soon, unless, indeed, he begin to ask, 'What am I doing wrong?' 'How did I stand?' 'How did I swing then?'

It is impossible to say how good a player a man may become; but every beginner ought, as much as possible, to play with better golfers than himself. He will unconsciously by that means aim higher. It should be his ambition to beat somebody, and, having done so, to attack a still stronger adversary. Many half-crowns will be lost in the process, but what of that? It is cheaper and pleasanter than to employ a professional coach.

In the early manhood of his golfing life, the earnest and promising player's mind is apt to be much exercised as to the weight, length, lie, and spring of his club. He will feel sure that a best club for his style is to be found, and to find it will for some time appear a matter of the last importance. After many experiments, he will be in possession of a mass of conflicting evidence, and a box full of clubs more remarkable than useful. From extreme hope and faith he will fall back into a condition of dogmatic unbelief. He will try to use any club – even the rubbish accumulated in his days of faith. Truth lies between these two extremes.

In the matter of lie, a tall player's club ought to be upright, a short man's flat. The reason is that for all sorts and sizes of men about 3 feet 6 inches is the proper length. That a longer club will not drive further, that a shorter one drives as far, is proved to be true. Theoretically, the long club reaches the ball with greater velocity, but as each inch adds to the difficulty of being accurate, it has to be taken easier. It is not your strong man who can wield a long club; on the contrary, it is your pocket Apollo, whose long driving is due to precision and neatness. An exceptionally short club, on the other hand, can be, and instinctively is, swung with much more force. The objection to their general use is that they break a man down, not so much from the fatigue of over-exertion as from the loss of self-control which results from it.

As for weight, so long as the specific gravity and the absolute weight of the head are both greater than these qualities in the ball, the carry will not be affected. Within these limits the lightest club will drive the longest ball, because it can be swung more swiftly than a heavy one (with what lightning accuracy one sweeps off daisy heads with a walking stick!). The danger with a very light club is that muscles having so little strain are apt to grow frisky and wanton. Theoretically, therefore, a heavy club ought to steady a wild, pressing player. It does not do so. It ought to act as a bit in his mouth. He takes it in his teeth. Practically, the golfer with an ambition for lead handicaps himself terribly. He cannot play easily in proportion to the weight of his weapon, for part of his ambition is sure to be to drive a long ball. This he will do occasionally; but he must hit perfectly clean, or else make an egregious foozle. There is no reserve force in him if he sclaffs. His club sticks in the mud, or is twisted out of his hand. To avoid the ground he is apt to top. Sometimes, when he does hit clean, the club runs away with him to the right or left. And all this on account of a crude, erroneous idea that the heavier the club the further it will drive. It is a mistaken idea, otherwise the man who could swing a 16-lb hammer would beat the record. It is evident that even Goliath would have made a very feeble shot with such a club or with his own; but with a Philp he might have out-driven the champion.

The spring of a club has more to do with comfort than with carry. Nobody likes stiff shafts. Many charges are laid at their door; the only just one is that they jar the hands. Each man will drive, not further, but better, with the club he likes best. A 'fozy' handle will do very well if you have a sweeping, scythe-like swing. If your style is jerky, such a shaft, or one with the spring under the rind, will prove itself useless to you at once; the club or the jerking must be abandoned. For all kinds of forcing players (those who let in when they get to the ball), the spring must be confined to the neighbourhood of the skeer. If you wish to compel yourself to drive easily, buy a 'wobbly' club; it will either teach you or top your ball. It is pleasanter, however, to play without a master. In short, my advice is – use a stiff club, whatever your style, with just enough elasticity to make the ball go off sweetly, and give up all idea that spring here or spring there will make you drive further. If you don't want to abandon this notion, no matter. Your club with an ideal spring may drive further on account of your confidence in it.

CHAPTER FOUR

Of Peculiarities and Faults

THERE IS a general – I might say universal – tendency among golfers to exaggerate the importance of style. From the best to the worst, when off their driving, they begin at once to alter something, assuming that the cause is to be found in a wrong stance, grip, or whatnot. And yet the experienced know well enough that their driving will never come back so long as they pursue this line of research. Style, in other words, is not nearly of so much importance as accurate hitting. Take a batch of first-class players, and we find that they all drive practically about the same distance, notwithstanding infinite variety in their way of doing so, and even greater differences in physique. It is usual to attribute the powerful driving of small men to the excellence of their style; if this be the cause of it, how does it happen that there are big men twice as strong, and with as easy swings as their little rivals, who as often play the odds after the tee shot as not? A batch of second-class players drives, on an average, some ten yards shorter than those who can give them a shade of odds (I do not include those who are second-class because they are beginners, or incurably careless). The same slight superiority

86

exists in the approaching of first over second-class players; and I am inclined to believe that this is also true in regard to putting, although it is the fashion to credit many bad drivers with skill in this department. Where are those fine putters on the ladies' green? How is it, when there are prizes there for men, it is some golfer known to fame who usually wins? No. Strength and style are of minor importance compared with accuracy. I do not mean that the first is of no value at all; but to ordinary physiques of five feet six inches up to giant-hood it gives no advantage, except from bunkers and bad lines. Even from these a Hercules is not necessarily the best. Precision is the main thing. When a man's eye is in he may address the ball in a dozen different ways with the same result; when it is out, no shifting of position will mend matters. First-class play is compatible with ugly style. A third-rate biceps may drive a long ball; but a second-class combination of hand and eye will prevent a man being both far and sure. To be a steady player, a man who finds he cannot hit a screamer every time must either play more easily or more coarsely, the latter preferable. Men learn their position instinctively. Watch an eminent golfer in the prime of youth, a prudent liver, or not old enough to be affected by imprudence, driving against, perhaps, a stronger man, who either never did aim exactly, or whose more delicate machinery is a little shaken by the wear and tear of life. How coarse and schlaffy the latter's shots are by comparison! One drives like a new hansom, the other rattles like an ill-built or old four-wheeler.

As we are accustomed to see dissimilar swings producing about the same result, so, on the other hand, cases of the exact converse are not uncommon – cases of two men with apparently the same style, one a powerful driver, the other incapable of sending the ball a hundred yards. Here comes a player who gets his hands under the club, swings it over his head, stands with the ball close to him, and yet sends it flying. Behind is another, his exact counterpart, except in the matter of results. Why is this? Why is the one a good player, the other not? If we take up a club of the first man, it is found to be very upright. Why he adopted this lie, whether by accident or on purpose, matters not. There it is, and he plays well, because his style is a natural product of a single-minded concentration on hitting clean. The duffer got his swing in another way, namely, by mimicry. The copy is fairly good, but not quite exact. The hands are Esau's, but not the club, which, being flat, compels him to add some movements not indulged in by his master. He has to bend down to adjust its head behind the ball, to rise during the swing, and subside again at hitting time. Not that this omission in the copy of externals matters much. His play would be no better with his ideal's club, because they differ utterly in their thoughts. The one thinks of hitting, the other about his manner of threatening to do so. Here is another good driver coming up to the hole where we critics are standing – another with an ugly style, as anything with peculiarities is called. He stands with his feet far apart – stands 'open' – and swings round his biceps, not his neck. Why is he driving well, and his partner and reflection so badly? Again a flaw in the copy gives a hint as to the origin of the leader's peculiarities. He has his hands very much under the club and at the same time exceptionally near the ground, whilst the other is evidently proud of his 'proper' grip. The intelligent onlooker (if I may be allowed so to speak of myself) retires a little off the course to drive imaginary balls, to discover that, given this particular grip, the rest follows as a natural consequence, and to speculate that probably the leader accidentally took this grip when he began to play, and thought no more about it.

The most natural manner in which to address a ball is, of course, to stand with legs straight and firm, and with no more stoop of the body than is absolutely necessary to enable the player to see it with straight eyes. But golfers, good ones, in the laudable endeavour to stand well away from the ball, acquire in great numbers the habit of stooping forward more than is necessary. These instinctively apply a corrective. For instance, some bend their knees. There are extremists who even stoop so far forward, and have cancelled the effect of doing so to such an extent by bending their knees, that they would fit a chair if placed behind them when driving. Some of the stupid imitators of these think the secret lies in the stooping, some in the knee-bending, with bad golf as a result in either case. Other good players, who stoop over their work, keep their bodies steady and their grip of the ground firm by placing the left foot nearer the line of fire than the right. They stand as in Fig. 3 – exaggerated. Some of the stability given in the line of fire by keeping the feet apart is thus used to prevent falling in. One of the best – if not the best – players in the world at the present moment in this way cancels the bad effects of his stooping forward to his work, and, as might be expected, at the sacrifice of a little of the straightness which a 'square' stand gives. At this moment his miserable imitators swarm on every golf green in the Lothians. They all copy his peculiar stance, some have grasped some other point; not one has improved his game. They have a little of Pygmalion's art; not one of them can animate their work. The ass of fable dressed like a lion they address like one. When the beast brayed he was betrayed; so it is when they swing.

Some day we may have a great player who has fallen into the habit of cancelling his stoop by placing his right foot near the ball, his left back (why not?), and then there will be a revolution among the mimics.

The examples of mimicry I have taken are of imitators of eccentric styles. Those who make copies of the orthodox swing are not so common, although there are pretty players who miss as often as not. Most who try it make an unrecognisable caricature, which is not to be wondered at, as caricature of persons with no salient feature is very difficult. Some again, who try to learn golf on imitative principles, have merely an imaginary ideal. In their case one can only infer from their exceeding bad play that they aim at a style instead of at a ball. Under this head come those who secretly determine to jerk instead of sweep the ball away, either through ignorance or stubbornness, or both. The ignorant flounder on, misdirecting their energy because they never have tried to strike in the right way; the stubborn, because they often jerk a long ball, and prefer the sensation to the gentler joy of feeling it slip away almost by itself, which a proper shot gives. The latter are hopeless. Golf is not a game for men who find more pleasure in brute force than in the exercise of skill.

It is usual to attribute peculiarities, whether of good or bad players, to their only having taken to the game late in life; but this neither explains them, nor is it quite in accordance with the facts. It is true that there are more artlessly artful players amongst those who have been on the green more or less since they could handle a leadless club two feet long, but it is quite a mistake to suppose that a man who takes his first lesson after his beard has grown, or even when the hair has all flitted from the top of his chin, is too old or too set or too something ever to swing easily. Why it is more exceptional for him than for the other to do so, is due to another cause. The boy begins differently from the man. He lets fly, indifferent as to a hit or a miss; or, rather, he means a clean, swishing, smashing blow. All others, from a glober to a fair shot, are merely misses, to which he pays no attention. They do not put him out; he expects them, and does not count the proportion of them to good shots. The bad ones do not matter, for his pleasure is to drive balls, not to play holes. Hence his style is quite free. A man has not patience for this. Just as the boy finds a round monotonous, so the man aims at striking steadily, leaving the rest to develop later.

It thus appears that the chances in favour of the former having a free style when he grows up almost amount to certainty, and yet, except that he has acquired a certain amount of skill, the boy beginner, as soon as he is old enough in mind to settle of his own accord to match-playing (I do not include those little boys who are forced into double harness with their fathers) is in the same position as a grown-up beginner. The man playing his first shot, and the golfer of (say) twenty-one, are equally ignorant of how much or how little it is safe to play consciously. The former thinks of what he is doing from the first, the latter begins to do so about this time of life. Either may go astray, or either may discover the golden mean before becoming set in the tricks they have excogitated. If this were not so, there would be fewer of those boy players who are expected to do wonders in two or three years, who at eighteen can beat anyone, and who at one-and-twenty disappear, either for ever, or to come to the front after an interval, with or without peculiarities, according as they used or abused their newborn consciousness. A perfectly unconscious style in a grown man is very rare. It will oftenest be found among professionals whose education does not tempt them to think. There is one illustrious and venerable champion of whom it is proverbial that not even a whole round of bad shots can tempt him to consider his position. 'I've missed the ba',' is all he says. To hit it again, is all he tries. It is wonderful how soon he succeeds, too – much sooner than if he were to begin asking why.

When a man first attempts to play, he is stiff and awkward indeed, but he has no mannerisms. They begin to show after his first breakdown, and after each succeeding one a mark is apt to be left on his game. When that is full-grown and set, the cicatrices of old wounds remain as excrescences, which, unless inconvenient, are better not excised. There is a risk of hurting the constitution of our golf if the operation is attempted. But as when an ankle has once been sprained, it is inclined to give way occasionally, so people with 'wonderful' styles are apt to crack unexpectedly, and when out of practice take a long time to come into their game.

Some people are lucky enough to have developed their abnormalities on non-vital spots. Though ugly, the ball yields as readily to their style as to something more elegant. You strike your shoulder, your thumb or thumbs are down the shaft, you bend your knees, shuffle with your feet, get your hands so far under the club that a full swing is impossible, etc., etc. These things will give no trouble. But if by playing for a pull, by gripping the club in a way that, although become natural, was acquired at a time when there was a wrong conception of how to make a ball fly, etc., you are wild and uncertain, there is nothing for it but to begin again. It is of no use to attempt patching; other faults have grown up alongside of the original one. They were necessary to put life into it at all. Say, for instance, you have a nipping style. You realise that, in consequence, your driving is short. It is useless to force yourself to follow the ball; you will only top. Stance, grip, and attitude have adapted themselves to the conditions originally imposed. There is nothing for it but contentment or a fresh start. For the latter, experience gives you an advantage over the real beginner. You know the true theory, viz., to stand opposite the ball and sweep it away by describing a true radius, on which it is a point. At first you will flounder, miss, and be uncertain; but a new and better game will grow to its full strength at last.

If we consider the plausible and insidious means by which these tricks insinuate themselves into a golfer's affections, it is not so much to be wondered at that he is conquered. By their aid he finds himself suddenly steady, able to beat adversaries previously dreaded, and to win handicap electroplate with strokes to spare.

At first they do not even shorten driving, the diseases taking some time to get into the system and cripple the other members. By the time they have done so, it is too late to get rid of them. The player works through stages of foozling, and, after as long a period as it would have taken to be a pretty golfer, he comes out a robust cripple, ungainly, although perhaps strong. This is the prognosis in the most favourable cases, but some would-be golfers are restless in the use of remedies. They employ device after device, add fault to fault. No sooner is their driving weakened by assimilating one, then another, and yet another, infallible 'steadier' presents itself, and is accepted, till at last there is not a chance of their cleanest-hit ball going more than fifty yards. These call themselves the steady old players. Steady, indeed! They top and puff just as often, if not oftener, than those who have acquired their game with less prejudice. They are steady only because it does not matter to their partners whether they hit or miss, and straight, because wildness is not appreciable in very short distances. Any morning we can see men out aiming at a style instead of at a ball. A trial swing now and then, especially before starting, may do no harm. There are even good players who indulge a good deal in the amusement. Them one can distinguish from the deluded creatures who are teaching themselves styles by the free thoughtless way in which they let out. The others – earnest, careful, apparently concen-trated on the blade of grass in front of them – do not hear 'Fore – stop that – hurry up,' shouted behind them; for their mind is busy committing to memory their last patent gyration. If the fools would but reflect on a certain passage of Scripture they might learn that neither leopard nor golf spotting can be managed by taking thought, and that thought will not add cubits either to their stature or to their driving. From the latter it will take some off.

These remarks do not apply to the petty variations in their style which many, or most, golfers are conscious of from day to day. Little vagaries are not part of us. Our knowing of them proves them external. If not made a serious point of, they do no harm. One of them will amuse for a round or so, and being the only thing which, for the moment, divides our attention with the essential of aiming, it may even improve our driving, and then be forgotten, modified, or smoothed out. The points under discussion are so superficial, or even imaginary, that no one notices them but ourselves. They are quite another thing from playing in the Morris, or the Fergusson, or the Fernie manner, which is amusing as tomfoolery, but, taken seriously, bob as he will, can never make a man a golfer.

Even minor sensations, too earnestly attended to, may, however, do a great deal of harm. When, by patiently keeping his attention fixed on hitting, the golfer has got into his best driving form, he is tempted to luxuriate in the sweet balls; to note how he gets his shoulders into the work; or how he feels like a whipcord, from the point of his toe to the head of his club; or, how, without effort, his palms feel glued to the rind of the club; and to determine that in future these joys shall be repeated every shot. Fool! He might as well expect to repeat the pleasure of appeased hunger by a second dinner, or make a pleasant dream more vivid by wakening. Pursuing these agreeable sensations he will lose them, and go off his game besides. Disappointed, he will return to the drudgery of hitting the ball, when lo! Some, or all of them come back too. Again he will be off in pursuit of the will-o'-the-wisp, and again break down. It takes long, long experience to convince a golfer that he must give up all the pleasures arising from a shot, except that caused by results, if he is to drive far and sure. Imitating one's own style is only less bad than copying a neighbour's. 'Know thyself' may be good philosophy; it is bad golf. Some players remain with the marks of sensation-hunting on their style for life. For instance, A. makes himself knock-kneed when he addresses the ball. Once, long ago, when he drove a beauty, there was a feeling of gripping the ground with the balls of his big toes. If you question him warily, he will tell you the year in which, and the hole at which, the sweet shot was made, that he has grown knock-kneed in endeavouring to repeat. B. sits down, because once, when he had a habit of falling forward (very likely he now falls back), it restored his game. C. turns in his toes because it cured him of swaying his body. Of course, it was stopping swaying, not standing like a crab, which restored his driving; but he did not know at the time what he was doing wrong, and so he has made a fetich of his toe, which, he thinks, is the god of driving. I know a golfer who does all these things, and a good many more. In his case they have long ceased to have any meaning or effect upon his play. They are like labels left adhering to our travelling-bags – records of former trips.

Besides the innumerable kinds of missing to which we are liable, certain players get into a way of driving exceptionally high or unusually low. Those who have acquired the latter peculiarity are not, like their opposites, dissatisfied, although they ought to be; for, of the two, they are likely to be the worse players. The high driver is inclined to be impatient at finding himself always playing the odd; but the other, although never steady, is reluctant to part with his reputation for length from the tee, and therefore seldom reforms. Nor is it so easy for him to do so as for the other, whose fault is due to simpler causes.

High driving is the result of too upright a swing. I do not mean that the onlooker sees the club go over the player's head, or anything of that sort; but he may detect that the club reaches, and also follows the ball at too steep a gradient. The typical high driver has a neat style – a little too easy, perhaps. He stands open, and with the ball too much opposite the right foot, on which he very decidedly leans his weight. The position makes it difficult for him to take a sweep back near the ground, and his easy, flipping swing tends to make the departure more abrupt still. Of course, many a skyer does not stand in this way. So much the better for him; he will have less trouble in describing a full segment of a circle, and of a larger one. It is not the position, but the way of coming down on the ball which skies it. A man standing for a pull, and pressing, often skies. If he asks his caddy how that was, he will say, 'You swung too quick,' so he did, but in this case quickness was the result of lifting the club too straight up, in his hurry to be back. I have often noticed that when a long, pulling shot is intended, the sky can be foretold if the player place himself with the ball less opposite the left foot than it should be for a bow-shaped raker.

In driving low, it is essential that the weight of the body rest more on the left than on the right leg, and that the hands pass over an imaginary line between the eye and the ball, in advance of the club head. If he is in the habit of standing square to the line he is going, it will be observed that a low driver has his ball more nearly opposite his left foot than is orthodox. This manner of address is not the cause of his abnormal trajectory, but a correction necessary to make his scheme of hitting succeed; as his hands are to pass over the ball before the club head (not at the same instant, as in the case of a true driver), he must thus stand behind, because if he did not, there would be no room between his grip and the ground for the club to continue its course after impact. By standing behind, the limit of arm's reach is touched immediately the ball is struck, and the hands sweep up to the level of the shoulder, leaving room between them and the ground for the club to follow. There would be no objection to this mode of driving, so efficient when it comes off, were it not bristling with difficulties. For one thing, a hook must be expected from time to time. The ball is too near the extreme point to which it is possible to sweep the club along the line of fire, the point at which the hands must do one of three things – stop altogether, rise towards the level of the shoulder, or sweep around the body. The first contingency has nothing to do with golf. If the hands are at the rise before the ball is reached, so is the club, and we have a skimmer off the horn, or a top. If they are kept down to prevent it, the club must sweep round and hook the ball. To see that this must be so, take an exaggerated case. Let the player stand normally – that is, parallel to the line of fire; but let

the ball be placed as far in front of the left foot as it ought properly
to be behind it. By leaning well on to that leg, it may be driven
straight, but it would be easier to drive it at right angles. Low
driving is prone to deride it's votaries in another way. For them, a
topped, or a heeled, or a toed ball is the same thing as for others;
but woe betide the low driver if he take it thick! His adversary's
'sclaff' will send as far anything else, provided he has his grip firm.
A little grass and earth no more checks a club than a little skin a
razor. Let the other touch ground, and his ball will spout into the
air, and land twenty yards from the tee; or he may give a wrench,
turn his club, and drive away to cover point. His hands being in
advance of it, they are nearer to the ground than the club's length,
so that it jams, stops, and jerks the ball up feebly; or else it carves
out a new course for itself away to the right, round the gate the
hands have closed, and there is a raker to whatever country lies
in that direction. With a hook to begin with, and a shot like this
to follow, the player, after two long shots, may find himself again
at the tee. Instead of standing parallel to their intended direction,
low drivers, and those who are so foolish as to try to be against
wind, sometimes get rid of the risk of sticking in the ground by
standing for a pull. They sweep the ball round, the club passing
over the ground as does a scythe, instead of straight over it. The
great disadvantage of this expedient is its wildness. The ball must
go off at a tangent from the circular sweep, and there is only one
which is straight. For low driving an upright club is best. It is easier
to stand over it – an essential. If you play for a pull, the arc of
the circle described over the ground is larger, and the tangents at

which the ball flies off more nearly coincident with it. The lowest driving club is the putter, because it is so upright; but of course it is too short to carry far.

Getting both hands well under the club also produces a low carry, and fairly long shots against wind, or where the ground is favourable. But players in this style are not long drivers under ordinary circumstances. Indeed, but for their balls flying low they would be short, this grip, as already shown, making a free, full swing impossible.

Although short drivers are scarcely a class by themselves, it is convenient now to treat consecutively some of the causes of shortness not already incidentally mentioned. Amongst those who are born late into the golfing world (whose period of gestation has endured, say, thirty years), many deliberately confine themselves to a half swing. Very properly beginning with this, they put a check upon their growing suppleness, and trust to powerful clubs and clean hitting. There is much to be said in favour of such procedure. They sooner arrive at maturity, and they escape (by keeping back from them) all the man-traps laid for the long-swing hunter. A half swing will never enable a man to say that he has driven the longest ball on record – at least truthfully, which is doubtless different – but it is effective, and will last. What a slogger loses in carry by shortness of sweep, he nearly regains by tautness of muscle. The slogger has a great advantage in this too, in that he is never tempted to press through wounded vanity. If he is out-driven a little, what of it? Is it not wonderful that he should get so far? How strong he feels. Better still, how strong he is admitted to be. It is a simple proportion sum. A. drives 200 yards with one shot, B. 190 with half a shot; how much stronger is B. than A.? Whilst his biceps is being admired, A.'s, which is, perhaps, bigger, must remain in its sleeve; or if produced, what is it? Bad meat, evidently, to judge by the driving. A. may indeed, perhaps, be evidently a clumsy player, and his reputation for strength will, in consequence, be saved; but it is a poor alternative to choose between being an awkward Samson and a puny fellow. Of all short drivers the slogger is the happiest; whilst his converse – he whose swing is short after impact – is the most contemptible in the matter of strength. As I have before pointed out, no one notices where a man's club goes after hitting the ball. The reversed slogger is merely written down a fraud if he has broad shoulders. The onlooker will conclude that they are tailor-made. To make it worse, his driving is even shorter than the slogger's. For some reason, which I do not know, the second part of a swing is the more telling of the two. We have seen that if a man has not a first-class combination of hand and eye, he will not have a game at all if he aims at very long driving. At the same time, many err on the side of hitting too easily, especially at first. Both mind and muscle accustom themselves to a conception of how the thing is to be done, of which they never get rid. Once formed, it is of no use for them to hit harder, unless they make a fresh start altogether. These are usually neat players, who stand too near the ball. But it is no use to get further away. Their muscles have accustomed themselves to work in a certain way.

A common cause of short driving, apart from eye (of course, in these paragraphs I am speaking of players, not duffers), is a loose grip. There is a confusion of opinion as to how tight one ought to hold. One fine driver will tell you that he grasps his club lightly; another that he clings as firmly as possible. The difference of opinion arises from quality of hands, and it may be assumed that neither lets the club move in the least degree from the beginning to the end of a stroke. A soft, well-padded hand, or a strong one, is firm unconsciously; a bony one must hold tight; a weak, bony hand, no matter what its owner is otherwise, conduces to short driving. If it holds tight, other muscles become sympathetically too rigid, and the ball is nipped. If it holds naturally, the swing must either be easy, or else the club slips a little. All three conditions of matters produce short driving. The golfer with weak hands must learn to hold tight without telegraphing the exertion to other muscles – a very difficult feat – or accept shortish driving as his lot. If he does this, the second alternative – to hold naturally and swing easy – is the best to adopt. To the first he cannot settle, the third will rub and blister his hands.

CHAPTER FIVE

Of Temporary Faults

A MAN'S GOLF, like the rest of him, is subject to many temporary ailments. By simply living as usual, his body will recover; by golfing, his golf will. For colds, golf and biliousness, the less doctor's stuff we can do with, the better. Yet prescriptions used in moderation may hasten the restoration of health or game, if it is the right medicine. That is the danger. Young golfers have often a sad time of it from hitting hard in the wrong way. The common phrase, 'Putting your back into it,' misleads them. The experienced player understands by this that from his foot to his hand he is to be one springy, supple sapling – that he is to be all of a piece – the stronger muscles accommodating themselves to do the same work as the weak, the greatest power of the weakest being the limit of force required of the strong. The young player misapprehends what is meant, and puts his back into it as the blacksmith does wielding his hammer, or the athlete putting a weight. In consequence, he commits many fatal mistakes – falling forward towards the ball, back from it, or swaying sideways over the right leg in swinging back. These things are done in order to catch the ball a terrible thud. One has seen (or even felt) boys flicking peas off the backs of their hands. The peas would not fly as far if driven from the shoulder. A golf ball is, indeed, too heavy to flick; but it is equally too light to putt like a 16lb. cannonball. I have already warned the beginner against swaying sideways; no more need be said about that. The second time he is bitten with the desire to squeeze, there will be an epidemic of falling forward. He will not know what he is doing, but the consequences will be apparent – hitting off the heel, club-breaking, ground-thudding – particularly the first. Most likely his caddy will make things worse by bad advice; attacking the symptoms, not the cause of the disease. His caddy will say, 'Stand further away.' This sounds like common sense, but it is not, any more than taking a foot-rule to measure the height of a mountain would be. The player tries it, falls in more, and heels as much. Desperately, he stands so that the ball is two feet beyond his reach whilst addressing it. The result is the same. Evidently he is not too near. Cynically he gets quite close, and lo! There is an epidemic of toeing and more club-breaking. Now he thinks he has discovered a secret, viz., that toeing is to be cured by standing further away, heeling by getting nearer. With this valuable piece of knowledge he expects, in no time, to find a stance which will compel the middle of his club and ball to meet. But he does not, and never will, until, after long grief and pain, he comes back humbly to the point from which he began to go wrong. The worst of thumping at a ball with the weight of the body is that now and then – just often enough to lure on its victim – there will be a long wild shot; occasionally, even a long straight one – longer than any he has driven before, the ball happening to be caught with a sweep which has been quickened to reach it before the player has quite lost his balance.

A ball hit off the toe is usually pulled, and one off the heel skids to the right. When an experienced player hits in either of these ways, it is to be hoped that he will recognise them as accidents due to faulty aim, instead of asking, 'What am I doing wrong?' It is as foolish to attribute these occasional shots to style, as it would be were they complete globers. But all pulled balls are not off the toe, nor heeled ones off the heel. You may have an epidemic of either unstraightness without wandering from the middle of the club. Pulling in this way is due to grip of the hands having got out of proportion. The right may have got too much above the club, or the left too much below it. Nature, *i.e.* a free address and careful aim, will provide a remedy, if the matter is left in her hands. If not, the disease grows worse, till the player finds his elbow sticking up before him so much that he can scarcely see the ball if the left hand is at fault, whilst there will be symptoms of cramp in that wrist if it be the right. Sometimes heeling (I still mean skidding to the right off the middle of the club) may arise from too timid a care not to pull, consequent checking of the swing by pulling in the arms, or by throwing oneself back. If the golfer has done one of these last two things, he will be conscious of it after the shot. Not so if his heel is due to another cause – placing the ball too nearly opposite the right foot, and catching it, consequently, before the club head has got into the straight.

It is true that skidding to right or to left, hitting off the toe or off the heel, may come from actually being too near or too far from the ball; but if it is discovered that either is the case, it is, nevertheless, dangerous to *get* further away or nearer. Rather, for the next shot, one should shake himself loose, and address the ball without prejudice. To *get* nearer or further away is almost certain to demoralise driving altogether. The former stiffens the player till he feels like the poker swinging the tongs; the latter tempts him to crouch over his work, so that he cannot do it for fear of toppling forward.

Although getting nearer, or further away, are useless as devices for making the ball go straight, they are mistakes that one is constantly falling into. It is within most golfers' experience that suddenly, and unaccountably, they go off their game entirely. They become feeble, uncertain, and, above all, uncomfortable in their address. When such a breakdown occurs, the cause of it is often standing at a wrong distance. The player does not feel that he is wrong. The error has crept gradually and insidiously into his style. He has been unconsciously varying his distance, inch by inch. Not that a foot nearer or further than ordinary affects play. In fact, everybody varies at each shot in this respect; but there is a point at which one's game suddenly collapses. If the breakdown be complete, it is not easy to detect the cause of it, for the feeling that one is going to foozle is so paralysing that one is likely to go entirely to ruin beyond hope of recovery – for that day, at least. But there may be nothing more than an evident incapacity to make the ball go a respectable distance, however cleanly hit. If this is the result of standing too near, the player will presently notice that he is inclined to do one of several things in addition to driving feebly. For instance, swinging back, there is a tendency to strike the shoulder; but it is more particularly after impact that the consequences of a wrong stance will reveal themselves. The player will be inclined at one shot to throw himself back; at another, his swing may end with an uncomfortable twiddle. Some shots he will jerk, stopping the club altogether; or, being quite determined not to do this, I have seen a golfer actually break his shaft by striking his left shoulder. These are symptoms if the player laudably persevere in hitting with the middle of his club. Should he determine to let out at the ball whatever happens, he will flounder it off the heel. If he has crept too far away, and is covering the extra distance by stretching out his arms, there will be a tendency to swing over the head rather than round the neck. If he is stooping to reach it, he will be inclined to fall forward, to jerk into the ground, and fail to follow (which may cause him to imagine that his fault is a loose grip), or there will merely be a general sense of decrepitude, proving itself not imaginary, by short, puffy shots. If the player makes up his mind to let into it, he may hit off the heel, just as in the case of being too near, but with this difference, that he may make a fair drive, either straight or hooked – hooked, to his astonishment, off the heel. It is quite true that, standing too far away, a player may hit off the toe; but this is usually an isolated accident (caused by taking a careless stance), which will not be repeated unless he is foolish enough to apply a corrective next shot.

Sensible golfers, either of experience, or who have devoutly accepted my previous remarks upon caddies' advice, know the folly of forcing themselves to do, or not to do, these things when told they are standing too much in front, not letting their arms away, not getting their shoulders in, etc. They (the sensible golfers of both sorts) know from experience, or from this book, that direct surgical treatment is of no use, and that, although their caddies' comments are quite just, they are better to keep hammering on, leaving the cure to nature, than to attack the symptoms. If they are very sensible, it is, however, no harm that they should know the causes of these things. We get too much front (see Fig.1) when the sweep we picture ourselves giving the ball is concave, like a scythe-cut, instead of straight. It is very common to drift into this mental attitude towards the stroke. Our club describes a semicircle through the air. Why not another over the ground? Why not, indeed, when there is a feeling of greater power, too? There is nothing to be said against this so long as all goes well; but sooner or later there will be a wild shot or two, a consequent loss of confidence, exaggeration of the position, and a general breakdown. What the player should do under these circumstances, is to set himself to what ought never to have been abandoned – the sweeping of his club straight in the direction the ball is wanted to go. Let him not think of his feet; they will follow his intention.

When we are not letting our arms away, it is useless to begin pushing them out after the ball. It is rather the tie to nip it firmly and, above all, to remember that the best of our force must not be expended in swinging the club back. At once things will come right, unless one of the results already spoken of reveal that we are too near the ball.

We do not get our shoulders in when it is the idea to follow the ball upwards the instant it is struck. There is nothing more tempting than to do this. We feel that it is our place to lift it; that otherwise it must grub along the ground, which of course it would, were it not for friction, or gravitation, or some such thing which the golfer naturally forgets about, if he ever knew.

It is extraordinary, but nevertheless true, that the most serious, complete, and persistent breakdowns are due to elementary aberrations. Very often a long run of exceptionally steady play will force on us, in spite of previous experience, the conviction that at last we have discovered that will-o'-the-wisp, the secret of driving, and that, by remembering it, we will be steady for ever. We are temporary victims of the illusion which the bad player never shakes off at all, with this difference – that by certain extraneous expedients he hopes to play, and never does, whilst we, playing well, hope to stereotype the means by which we are doing it. Yesterday we were driving far and sure; today we are determined to play with hands and feet placed, and club swung exactly in the same manner. We do not quite get a hold of it; search, and break down; search more, and break down worse. There are few of us wise enough to learn, once and for all, the lessons here taught, viz. : – 1st, that as soon as any point of style is allowed, during the shot, to occupy the mind more than hitting the ball, a miss, more or less complete, will result; 2nd (and this is less obvious), that nobody can acquire complete uniformity. If we are driving well, do not let us trouble ourselves unduly about how it is done. Let us rather bear in mind that slight *nuances* of difference in grip, or stance, or swing, are of no importance. For instance, I am driving well, and cannot help observing that I have my hands more than usually over the club. Just because I have noted the fact, there will be, next time I take my stance, an inclination to alter this. It would be a mistake to balk myself. If we are not thinking of style at all, being too intent upon the match, there will be little variation; but if we are, let us give way to it, saying to ourselves, 'All right, do what you like about that – I am busy with the main issue.' I do not mean that we can over-swing or get into a constrained position with impunity; but there is no danger of extremes so long as differences of attitude, mental or bodily, towards the ball, are not expected to drive it. It will be within the experience of many, that when an adversary, after playing a few holes, explains that he feels he is going to drive well today, because he has hit upon the proper something or other, he ends by being an easy victim. But if he says, 'I feel that it does not matter how I go up to the ball,' we may be sure that nothing but good play will secure us the victory after a hard-fought battle.

It does seem as if, when a breakdown takes place from attempting to stereotype a successful style, nothing were simpler than to recover. But this is not always, nor, indeed, usually, the case. Of the best players it has often to be said for months that So-and-so is not playing well. Nay, a breakdown may last so long that a first-class player becomes an acknowledged second, and remains so for years or forever. This is not common case; but retrogression, more or less complete, of from a day to three months is. It seems as if periods of bad play ought never to last long. The player does not anticipate it. Nothing seems easier than for him to recollect the manner or manners in which he hit when steady. He tries for them, one after the other, and fails.

Although a shot is made in a moment, there are many which remain green in the memory, and of which the player can recall, long after the particular sensation, how his shoulders seemed to get into that one, his feet to grip the ground for another, his hands to have held the club as if made for it for another. A man has always a dozen pet shots in stock, to the sensations of which he tries (and fails) to return when a breakdown comes. Then he says, 'Never mind; perhaps I am thinking too much of how to hit, and too little of hitting.' This is sure to be true; but he still fails. During his spell of good play all the elements of driving, such as sweeping the ball away, placing the club behind it, etc., became second nature. During his period of style-hunting some vicious tricks have got grafted on to them. The name of these is legion. He may know, and be told by his caddy, that he is swinging too fast, without knowing that it is so, because he is lifting his club too straight up. A lack of confidence may have twisted him into some uneasy attitude, or (this is almost certain) he is hitting too hard, which he was able to do successfully when in form. It looks as if I were now admitting (what had already been denied) that there are a thousand and one things to remember at every shot. This is not so. The very reason of the continuance of the breakdown is that the player (although he tells himself he has) has not purged himself of these things. When playing well he swung swiftly and stood firmly, but within the limits of ease; now there are quickness and stiffness without ease, and, above all, impatience to recover.

At last he will humble himself utterly. He will give up mending his style. To his feeling, his swing will be short and stiff, his hitting weak and careful. The recovery will be rapid, but not immediate, as all this time he has been trying to make it. His lost confidence will cause many a miss; but after a round, or even less, there will be a recovery of fitness for freedom. He will by degrees tighten his grip, and let them have it. But let him take care. Let him beware of noting his symptoms, so that the way to do it may not escape him again. If he does so, another relapse is certain. It is only when each shot is treated as a separate act, in no way guaranteed by previous good ones; when each time he addresses the ball his chief care is to hit it – not far, not in this way, not in that, but hit it; when how far it is to be struck is scarcely thought of; when, during the swing, there is no consciousness of how he is swinging – that there will be an almost continuous record of palpable hits. That nobody almost ever plays a dozen shots equally clean, exactly as far as each other, is because they cannot absolutely do this. The experienced player knows that his last shot was perfect because his mind was applied to it, and to it alone; and yet he cannot prevent himself from trying to make the next as good, not in the same way, but by repeating thc last. One can watch the process in any adversary who has played a strong, steady game for (say) half a round. He is thoroughly stretched, supple, confident, and consequently out comes one of those extra long shots. If you and he both leave him alone, he takes no heed, and other extra ones follow at intervals. But, if you are a cunning player, flatter him about his shot, point out that his next is as long, and, if he takes the bait, the third may be long too; but your experienced eye will detect that he has staggered and over-exerted himself to produce it. It is a question of your tact against his sense, whether you get him broken down altogether, or whether he returns to hitting steadily and without prejudice.

In conclusion, I will summarise the times we are in most danger of relapses. One is, as just explained, when we are in a particularly good vein of play. Pride goes before a fall. The slightest shade of retrogression from a perfection we have come to consider normal may make us impatient, or lead to an examination of the cause, and either impatience or examination is fatal. To be beaten in an important match, to be distinctly out-classed by a player not considered our superior, when playing our best game, is very trying. On the other hand, an uninteresting match, which we can win as we choose, may start us on a fatal course of experimenting. Lastly, after a long absence from the green the risk is great. There is a false axiom that a man cannot play well under these circumstances, which is often made true because it is accepted. We return to work expecting to do ill. We play carelessly. We hit hard, trusting to Providence before our muscles have got accustomed to their duties; and, in about three days, when our form ought to be returning, it is further away than ever. No wonder! For two days have been employed in acquiring vices. When a man has had a holiday, let him settle down to each shot as if a match or a medal depended on it, and his game, or a better one than he ever played before, will be his in no time. Men often absent themselves from the green because they have broken down. These usually recommence humbly, and find their game restored. All returning prodigals should do likewise. The folly of sowing careless shots on fallow ground, in the expectation of reaping good golf, is unspeakable.

CHAPTER SIX

Of Playing through the Green

AFTER AN accurate tee shot, the second has usually (a grumbler would say, sometimes) to be played from a light lie on soft sward, and is but a repetition of the first. Some people, however, maintain that you should hit as hard as possible from the tee, and take it easy through the green. The wisdom of this is doubtful. It seems to me to be better to hit boldly and with a will in both cases. To attempt to strike harder than hard is, for most men, to top, whilst softer than hard causes a heel or a draw. What club should be used through the green – driver, brassy, or spoon – may be left to individual sentiment. It is common to hear it said, 'I cannot use my play club through the green.' The answer to such nonsense is 'Learn, then.' But if a man says, 'I prefer my brassy,' then brassy let it be. He is probably the owner of one which happens to suit him well. It is very likely that, in six months, the favourite will be broken, three or four rejected copies will be lying in his box, a pet driver reigning in their stead. Between a driver and a brassy, or a long spoon, the difference is practically fanciful. It is another matter if a short spoon or a cleek is constantly used for full shots from clean lies. You may be sure you have to do with a poor player if he cannot use the proper club, and does not try to learn.

But, alas! the ball does not always lie well. Then brassy, cleek, iron, and niblick sprawl themselves fan shaped, derisively, before the mental vision, with a mark of interrogation after each. On the border-land, between good and bad lies, is the hanging ball. One of these with a face a yard or two in front of it, is a bad ball, which can only either be dunched along the ground a short distance with a brassy, or popped equally far with an iron. When there is no face in front, a hanging ball ought to go as far or further than another. Why it baffles many golfers is that they try to raise it instead of playing it downhill, leaving nature to raise it. A caddy will say, 'Turn in the face.' This is good advice if taken to mean that the club is to lie naturally towards the slope it is to drive down. If it is placed hopefully, in accordance with the general lie of the green, a shot similar to what results from turning up the face when the lie is normal must follow. A good general maxim for a bad lie is, when in doubt between two clubs, take the meaner. The violent do not take the hole by force. It is the patient who are rewarded. With a bad lie there is more need than ever of a firm grip and an exact aim. These are the means by which the ball can be forced. A violent swing and a terrific blow may force a clean ball, but a cupped one derides such treatment. There are bad lies and bad lies. Even a thick tuft of legitimate grass is not so bad as it looks. It will scarcely do more than leave a green mark on the club face. But these little sandy patches, half-bred between a bunker and a putting-green, are treacherous indeed. One little teaspoonful of sand taken with the ball, and your adversary gains half a shot. Beware of a cup, however small. If you expect to demolish it by means of a little extra powder, you are mistaken. If the higher side of this innocent little inch of slope is in front of you, the chances of a clean drive are very small – much less than if there is only a lump behind. A careful aim will slip you in between the latter and the ball. Clean balls, lying to you or from you ever so little, must be allowed for, if you are to go straight. These are very deceptive. Sometimes the declivity is not even noticed, and something else is blamed when we fly away off the line. The worst of bad lies are caused by a few sparse shoots of long, wiry grass. I do not know the botanical name of that diabolical stuff; most likely it is christened in a way which it would be impolite to write. These grasses, like cholera, are more virulent in autumn. I say, beware of a few of them. If there are many, the bad lie is self-evident, and we humbly take a niblick. But a few are just as fatal. They whip themselves round the shaft and arrest its progress, like the toasted cheese which clings to your feet in a nightmare, when you are within a hundred yards of the city of refuge, and the avenger at your heels. But bad lies have their bright side. Sometimes, by taking thought, one makes a shot, even with a niblick, which rejoices and surprises. They, moreover, make one grateful for a clean-lying ball. Best of all, the adversary may be the unfortunate. There are few more restful, hopeful, happy moments at golf than those in which he is hesitating about which club to use, cursing his luck, consulting his caddy, changing his stand. It is better even than to see him in a bunker or up against a fence. You know that it is any odds to one that he will take the wrong club, and that the loss of the hole will be due to his own fault. Up against a fence, one's joy is tempered by an uncomfortable feeling that Providence is interfering too much.

CHAPTER SEVEN

Of Bunker Play

BEFORE LEAVING that part of the game in which sending the ball as far as possible is desirable, it is necessary to consider for a moment a very painful subject – Bunker Play.

The mere appearance of a niblick suggests doubts and fear. Other clubs are graceful, smiling, elegant things. The niblick is an angry-looking little cad, coarse, bullet-headed, underbred. Its face looks up as if to say, 'I will raise the ball into the air.' Its smile is treacherous. It does fulfil its promise sometimes, but just as often it smothers its laughter in the sand, leaving you and the ball nonplussed.

No one is ever proud of his bunker play. Some men of strong shoulders are more successful with the niblick than others; but they do not glory in their strength. There are men who give up the hole when they find themselves in sand, preferring to pretend that they seldom get into any to more substantial advantages. So little is force exerted in a bunker regarded, that men who act thus are not credited with weak physique.

There is at the best little pleasure in niblick play. When you are compelled to ask for that implement, it is under a sense of humiliation at having put yourself into sand. Even if you get out, you are an unprofitable servant, not quite so far on with your work in two shots as you ought to have been in one. Perhaps the feeling nearest akin to pleasure derivable from a niblick shot is a partner's sense of relief when you get the ball out. This the player does not share. With the hopefulness inherent in the true golfer, he expected to succeed. Besides, the twenty yards or so the ball has travelled seem a small result, considering the extent to which his withers are wrung.

If there is small joy to be got from bunker play there may be great sorrow. The ball may not be got out in one shot. Indeed, after six it may be worse in than at first. This may entail nothing more than the giving up of the hole. But supposing your adversary to have played two or three more before you got in, how sickening! In medal play or a stroke match, in which you have backed your score against others, can anything be more awful than to feel a sovereign vanishing at each blow? It is a providential arrangement that a niblick is so coarse an implement. If it were a club that could scarcely be replaced, men would often add shame to woe by breaking it. But a shaft which can infallibly be replaced for a few shillings is useless as a safety-valve. On the other hand, a niblick is a formidable weapon of offence, and I have seen the life of an adversary, who counted the oft-repeated shots aloud, in serious danger.

It is worthy of observation that bad players are *ceteris* (*i.e.* muscles) *paribus* as effective in a bunker as the best. This is because nobody has any theory about his swing or his stand, or this or that, when addressing himself to a common ordinary bunkered ball. Every one simply thuds at it. Men who, on the green, must needs shuffle, bob, and writhe, each in their own manner, as much as if coming into the presence of the Llama of Tibet, the ball waiting for them as calm and stolid as he, will hit freely and naturally with the niblick. Another reason why one man is as good from an ordinary sand cup as another, is that the ball is best dislodged by a jerk. A lot of sand must be forced away with the ball, so that it is really a heavy object for the nonce. As we have seen, it is because it is not always so – because it is so light – because hard thudding will smother it – that skill in driving is an art, and not a mere question of strength.

Most bunkered balls, then, are best dislodged by a good coarse jerk. It is usual to take a full swing with a niblick; but my own opinion is that a half one is more effective, particularly if you use a light club. Whether a heavy or a light one should be carried may be left to individual fancy. The weight of the former makes up for any loss of applicable force.

Sometimes a bunkered ball presents peculiarities which make it unadvisable to apply the common thud. If there is a high face to loft, or if there is a mound of sand close in front of the ball, the shot to be described at page 140 is advisable. That miniature face in front is particularly apt to cause disappointment. If there is one behind as well, the player grasps at once the horror of the situation but not if all is clear in that direction. Yet if the ball be struck in the ordinary way, when there is a face only in front, it is as unlikely to be treated successfully as when entirely surrounded.

A mound behind, with flat sand in front, is not nearly so serious. By getting in front, and chopping down close to the ball, or simply by driving mound and ball together, satisfactory results may be expected. The above shot is also the only one that will do in a hard, deep, clay-bottomed bunker. If there is no face to get up, it is different. The ball lies then as well as if on the green, except (and it is a considerable exception) that the club cannot be placed behind it. Be cautious with a teed ball in a shallow sand bunker, however. It is very nearly a mad thing to take a wooden club. Even a cleek or an iron must be selected with much solemnity. But if there is a face to rise over!

CHAPTER EIGHT

Of Approaching

WHEN THE player's ball is within less than a driver shot of the hole, approaching commences, and new qualities – the sense of weight, how to weight it, appreciation of distance, etc., are called into requisition. The least amount of difference between driving and approaching exists when the distance is still so great that a full shot from a cleek or an iron is advisable. Some players find it easier to drive with wood than with iron; but this is not because the latter should be wielded in a different way. The difficulty is either sentimental, or due to some false attitude of mind. A feeling that an iron club will sink into the ground, or the opposite view, that it is more capable of cutting through it, may incline a man on the one hand to top, on the other to puff the ball. A man's iron shots may go too high because he lays the club unnaturally back, or because, looking upon it as more powerful than a wooden club, he, intending to hit harder, swings too quickly, therefore too straight up and down, therefore lofts too high. These results are not due to the clubs, but to the player's treatment of them. There is one real difference, however, between wood and iron. A golfer who is inclined to cut

Plate 9. Addressing for an approach shot.

the ball will find his tendency to swerve to the left greater with the latter, probably because of the more polished face. Long driving with iron clubs is the result of clean hitting, as with wood, except sometimes in the case of beginners, many of whom congratulate themselves on what should be a cause of regret and a hint that something is wrong – namely that they drive as far with a cleek as with a play club. This something is the possibility of treating the ball as a heavy object with a cleek, and so treating it effectively. A jerk with iron endows it with something of the elasticity of wood. But a jerker can never reach a first-class standard of steadiness. This will dawn on the beginner as he improves, and his jerks will be reserved for cupped balls.

The nomenclature of true approach shots – those requiring less than a full swing – is somewhat indefinite. Half, three-quarter, quarter, wrist shot, etc., mean each something to players who employ the terms, but they have no generally recognised manner nor status. It cannot be laid down that if a full shot goes a hundred yards, a quarter shot goes twenty-five, etc. Nor is there even an approximate law regarding the number of inches the club ought to be drawn back in order to propel the ball an equivalent distance in yards. All that can be done is to give a few general hints as to how to do it, and how not to do it. The sense of weight must be exercised and cultivated by each player for himself.

One rule, without exception, is that no ball however near the hole, should be played weakly. Even the shortest of all approaches – styme lofting – can only succeed if the ball is swept away, the grip tight, the muscles taut. A weak tap, however long or short the distance, will prove uncertain and disappointing. The length of swing, not the firmness of sweep should regulate the carry.

The attempt to play an easy full shot is generally recognised as a mistake, and most men consider it wiser to cover the distance with a drive from a weaker club, or an approach shot from a stronger. When it comes to these last, however, the folly of attempting to 'spare' is not equally acknowledged.

Longish approaches are sometimes attempted to be made by means of a half shot. That is to say, the player addresses the ball as in driving but shortens his swing by getting his hands more under the club than usual, and by keeping all the joints above the diaphragm rigid. This mode of play is scarcely worth cultivating. I do not mean that those who always drive in this way and in no other, or those who, being bad at full shots with irons, have adopted this style with them, ought to reform; but it is difficult to acquire as an occasional means for limiting the length of a drive. The muscles are apt to assert themselves in their usual routine, and a miss to result from the conflict of intention and habit. Nevertheless, half shots of this sort are frequently attempted with a cleek or an iron; but it is an indirect proof of their unsoundness that no one ever seriously tries to play them with a driver.

Unless under exceptional circumstances, to be considered presently, there are thus only two proper modes of approaching – by full drives from short clubs, and by what are called wrist shots. It will be found that the best players have no styles between these two. According to length of swing for various distances, they speak of quarter, half, three-quarter, or full approach; but these terms

Plate 10. 'Just within a wrist' (1).

are used for their own convenience, and refer merely to longer or shorter shots played in the same style. A half to them means a half wrist, not the half spoken of in the last paragraph. Beginners and others ought clearly to understand that whilst they ought to have one style for driving, whether with wood or iron, successful wrist play is a new departure, and that effective approaches cannot be manufactured out of fragments of a full swing.

What, then, is a wrist shot? For one thing, it is a shot which ought not to be played with the wrists. Their usual name misleads many a beginner, and causes him to flounder hopelessly for years. To use the wrists alone is so neat, comprehensible, and compact an idea that he grasps it at once. He is conscious that using one set of muscles and joints alone, his sense of weight is more delicate. It will not take him long to learn, although it may be years before he is convinced that this is not the way to do it. It would be less confusing if approaches were called ankle shots. The ancients called them knee shots. It is to be deplored that, for no obvious reason, a term so tutorial became obsolete when baffys and feathers were superseded. Properly these joints are brought more into play than the wrists.

Without wishing to direct attention too emphatically to one point, it is nevertheless true that the left wrist joint has no part to play in good approaching, and must be rigidly restrained from taking any. Men who are masters of the iron may say this is non-sense, and of course they would spoil their play by keeping that or any other point too much in view; but it may easily be noticed that such persons do keep that joint rigid, even although many of them give a preliminary flourish. I say many; but also it may be

Plate 11. 'Just within a wrist' (2).

noticed that, contrary to what is the case in driving, most do not. The rule is to put the club undemonstratively behind the ball, and at once to strike. To the tyro, then, if he is getting on well, I would say nothing; but if he is not, a perfectly stiff wrist will do much to reveal the secrets of approaching. Of course, too much attention to and misapprehension of this point (as of most golf secrets) may lead to faults. The player may make wrist-bending impossible by getting his hand under the club, or by laying the spare end of the shaft along his arm. He is also apt to tuck his elbows into his sides, and play as if they were strapped to his body, or, going to the other extreme in order to give his left arm free play, stick it out so far that the swing must be a slice. The proper position is easy – the left hand well over the club: there is to be no effort even if the muscles fail to do the work of bone.

Probably an excised joint would not be missed. But it is effort, not elasticity of wrist, which would give the maimed man an actual advantage. As a rule, players talk and think more about the position of the right than of the left hand in approaching. They discuss whether the thumb ought to be down the shaft or over it, tight or loose. So long as the elbow is close to the body, these things do not seem to be matters of the slightest importance. Approachers of equal skill indulge in all the variations. Indeed, some are not constant to their own fancy, sometimes having the thumb over, sometimes down the shaft. As in driving, the position of the right hand is a point too much attended to, that of the left too little.

Whilst, as we have seen, in driving a good deal of licence is allowable in the matter of stance – some players placing their feet parallel to the line of fire, some with their back a little to it, some with their face – the last is the only proper position for approaching. One has but to take a club in hand, and the necessity for this will make itself evident. Let the experimenter actually pause after swinging back (say) two feet. Standing in the proper way, there will be no tendency on the part of the club to waver from its line. But let him stand square, or in front and swing back the same distance: the position is stiff, and it is difficult to avoid describing a loop at the beginning of the return journey.

Assuming that the player has accepted the principle that the length of his approaches is to be regulated by distance of swing, he ought soon to become pretty accurate for distances from twenty-five to one hundred yards, one would think. Why men remain so uncertain is due to many causes. For one thing, they do not adhere to the principle. At short distances they are inclined to swing easily, which really means flabbily, and with a loose grip, or else to swing too little, and apply more force. At long distances they hit extra hard. Now, to acquire accuracy, it must be realised that at all distances the grip must be firm and the muscles taut; and that the ball will be reached with more impetus, and therefore hit harder for every inch the club is drawn back. The temptation to over-stiffen oneself, and force for a long approach, can only be resisted by careful watching. There is a natural tendency to cover a little more distance by an ounce more of exertion – by quickening of the swing, rather than by an inch more of it – leading, if not checked, to a habit of jerking, which renders the regulation of distance impossible. This is a real difficulty; others are either self-made or due to ignorance. One of the latter, almost universal with tyros, is to attempt to scoop the ball up into the air. Nothing is more common than to see the face of the iron after the shot, held up as if for alms, whilst the ball is trundling along the ground. Let the golfer ever remember that it is the lie of the club, not a turn of the wrist, which is responsible for the loft. Some men can never make up their minds whether they intend to take the ball clean, or to shave off a little turf with it. Having made a good shot with turf, they regulate the swing accordingly, till (a foozle must happen sometimes, however one plays) they take too much, or make a good shot clean. It matters very little whether a player takes ground with him or not; but it becomes serious if he is hazy as to his intentions. Again, the custom of using sometimes a heavy iron, sometimes a light one, sometimes a cleek, sometimes trying to run the ball, sometimes to loft it very high, postpones the day when comparative certainty may be attained. What the player ought to do is to decide what club he will habitually use; whether he will take turf or not; note the height of his loft when he hits as he means to, and stick to this as his standard. This done, there ought to be nothing to think of, in nine shots out of ten, except the length of swing necessary to cover the distance, and accurate hitting.

The player who can make lofts from normal lies to within a yard or so of where he means, even although he foozles in complicated situations, overruns ticklishly-placed flags, or fails to loft steep hillocks, is more effective than he who has as many styles, and as many irons, as there are holes in the green. A showy shot

Plate 12. Sixty yards from the hole (1).

which comes off should be hailed as 'good fluke,' and its player ought to thank Providence instead of smiling round complacently. Do I mean that one ought merely to thwack at the ball despairingly whenever it is in a difficulty? Certainly not. But if it seems feasible to play a fairish shot in a normal way, that is better than to attempt anything gaudy. If something exceptional must be tried, let it be as slight a modification as possible of orthodox play – let it be a deduction from it. Out of a cup one's natural inclination is to try to spoon the ball, from long grass to mow it, against wind to force it. The golfer ought to ignore cups, grass, or wind as natural features, reducing each to terms of yards. There are very few lies which it is not the best policy to treat in this way. So long as there is an even chance of getting the ball to within twenty yards of the hole by ordinary means, fancy shots ought not to be undertaken, for there is little doubt that the latter oftener fail than succeed. I do not mean that proficiency in the showier kinds of approaches is impossible. Many a player makes himself the talk of the green for a season by his marvellous power of lofting a ball so as to lie where it alights: but invariably the iron with which this is done breaks; or, in some other way, the proud owner of it loses his abnormal skill, and the last state of that man is worse than the first. His practice of approaching in the simplest way has been abandoned for this more fickle masterliness, and you see him topping, puffing, missing, with cleeks, irons, mashies, in the vain effort to strike out a new road to glory.

It may seem unnecessary to insist so much upon anything so self-evident as the necessity of adhering to one simple mode

Plate 13. Sixty yards from the hole (2).

of approaching; but it is requisite, unless preaching is vain. The temptation to indulge in variations is almost irresistible. The devil seems to hover over the golfer, and ever to whisper in his ear, 'Try this,' or 'Try that.' He listens to the tempter. It would be so nice if he did chop it up in the air out of that hole, and lay it dead. 'It may rise,' he thinks, 'whilst it will only look like a fluke if it scuffles up within holing, played in the ordinary way.' He yields, tries, and odds are it goes but a few yards, eliciting the well known cry of repentance, 'I ought not to have tried it.'

Take another case. The hole is just beyond a bunker. Playing properly, you must run past. The temptation to lay the iron back, or to put a spin on from the heel, or to deaden the fall by hitting off the point, or to employ some new system lately patented, is very great. That it is not the game is proved by the secret joy experienced when an adversary announces his intention of making one of these showy attempts. Even in a score game, six shots behind and three holes from home, the flames of hope begin to flicker in your sulky bosom.

Although rarer than golfers make them, there are occasions when fancy shots are worth trying. For instance, if a bunker is between us and the hole, danger beyond it, and no chance of even a half unless we are in in two, the ball must be lofted high or else spun. Some players, in these circumstances, use a loft iron in the usual way, others try to lay back an ordinary one. Both shots are difficult; but, to my thinking, that with the specially made club is the riskier. It must strike the ball with absolute precision. If taken too thick, the shape of the club makes it dive into the ground, and

Plate 14. Lofting high (1).

Plate 15. Lofting high (2).

puff the ball a yard; too clean, it will skim it a hundred yards with
the force that would have lofted it fifty. Laying back the iron is not
so uncertain if properly done. One way not to do it is to play an
ordinary approach shot, the face of the club pointing upwards. A
top is as certain as if, in driving off the tee, you pose the lead instead
of the sole of the play-club on the ground. Properly, the laying
back is not done by rolling the club over on its heel, but by putting
it on the ground in advance of the hands, and (this is the important
point) drawing it back almost along the ground. So low must the
swing be that if made full (which it never is for this shot), it would
be round the waist instead of over the shoulder. In this shot the ball
must be swept away, not cut or nipped. There will be a spin on the
ball, but woe to the player who attempts to increase this spin with
a turn of the wrist! There is no reason why great certainty in this
shot should not be attained. Indeed, it is a favourite with many at
from fifty to twenty yards, but its application is limited to clean lies,
and lies in soft grass, as is the use of the lofted iron. It is useless to
try it on a hard green, still more so from a bad lie. However tightly
the club be grasped, the attitude is not adapted for forcing a ball.
Attempted in a bunker, the result is almost invariably disastrous. A
tablespoonful of sand is too much for the strongest arms.

There is another fancy shot which differs utterly from the last
except in respect of results. It may be played at all times instead
of the other, whilst from a bad lie it is the only way I know of
to loft a ball. In this shot the cub is lifted more nearly straight
up than in a normal one, crashing into the turf behind the ball.
But there is more to attend to. Why many fail at this blow is that,

when Mother Earth interferes with the completion of the segment of their circle, they submit. To succeed, the player must follow the ball, not in the same curve that he swept down on it, which is impossible, but as best he can. This best will be an ellipse. (See this shot illustrated, Plates 14 and 15.) It is wonderful how beautifully the enemy will spout into the air. Among all these shots, which are loosely described as wrist shots, this is the only one in which the wrists legitimately come into play. To get the club, as it were, round the corner, after the ground is reached there must be a twist from them. The disadvantage of the shot is that, even from good lies, the distance is extremely difficult to regulate. It will fail altogether if anything but a strong blow be struck. Still many will remember the wonderful accuracy Jamie Anderson acquired in it some years ago, hitting a full blow at all distances, and regulating the length of his loft by the inches of turf he took behind the ball. In a bunker this shot is also useful (a niblick, or mashy, of course, being the weapon employed), better perhaps than the ordinary dig. By it a ball may, if necessary, be lofted higher, and, what is still more to the point, it will often be got out of a deep cup, in which the common thud would merely bury it.

When the ball is close to a straight face, a shot somewhat like this last may, in desperation, be attempted. The club is lifted nearly straight up and brought down with a crash an inch or so behind it, as if the only intention were to split open the ground. There should be no attempt to follow. Sometimes (I say emphatically sometimes) the ball will spout up into the air in a marvellous manner. This shot cannot come off except out of loose sand.

Plate 16. Running it with an iron (1).

A style of approach often employed is running the ball with the iron, either along the ground, or very little above it. When this is attempted, it is customary to turn in the club face. By so doing, the player gets the sentiment of his intention; but that is all. The turning of the iron alone will not run a ball. The essential thing is that the player be well over the ball, and his hands slightly in advance of it – in fact, just as far from the 'juste milieu' at one side, as they are at the other when he attempts to 'lay back' the iron. (See Plate 16) It is necessary to point out that the position of the hands, not the turning in of the club, is the essential thing in this shot, because, although doing the latter inclines one to the former, the one is quite possible without the other.

(Let me observe parenthetically that merely turning the toe of a club, in or out, is of no effect in any shot, except to convert a properly made tool into a bad one. Placing the club out of its proper position is simple folly, unless it be part of the result of the mode of address, not an isolated contortion.) Our player, then, has taken his position for a skimming approach. His hands are well in front, the club face turned in – not to keep the ball low, but partly because it now naturally lies that way, partly because that way of resting it makes it a more upright club for the nonce – and uprightness, we have seen, is conducive to low trajectory. A common mistake is now to jerk – the thing, of all others, which ought not to be done. Jerking raises a ball. The club should rather be dragged, the wrists rigid, the grip excessively firm. From rough ground near the hole, or on a bad putting-green, this shot is very useful. Many prefer it to an ordinary loft at shortish distances, the

Plate 17. Running it with an iron (2).

Plate 18. Running it with an iron (3).

latter being more difficult within, say, thirty yards than when the player has further to carry. There are some who employ it for all approaches, and with good effect too. These you may recognise by their stance, which is often square or even in front.

There are four clubs used for ordinary approach work – the putter, the cleek, the iron, and the mashy.

The first, of course, can only be used on very flat ground. Long putts, and the putters thereof, are much despised. A putt of sixty yards laid dead causes anger or laughter, according to the temper of the adversary. But I am bound to say that those who are well practised in 'skelping' often call forth the exhibition of one or other of these forms of emotion. The worst of this mode of approaching is that, sooner or later, it undermines the constitution of the most delicate and valuable club in the set; whilst to carry two putters – one as a whipping-boy – is unwise. They cannot be made exactly alike, and, even if they are nearly so, hesitating between the two at intermediate distances is apt to put a player's putting powers out of gear. Cleek approaches do not lay your respectability open to doubts like long putts, which have the same odour of meanness as the 'sneak' of boys' cricket. Although for the most part low, they are not absolutely crawling things. They have one distinct advantage over iron approaches. The cleek, lofting low, can be used at greater distances than the iron, thus bridging over that rather wild country which lies between a full cleek or spoon shot and the approach proper. But the cleek has little else to recommend it as against the iron, which, played with equal skill, is in most circumstances more effective.

The least hillock will catch and kill a cleek approach, whilst, even in the absence of such obstructions, the run at the finish is necessarily so long, that the chances of stopping or turning bumps are greatly increased. Some people will object that there is as much chance of a lucky as of an unlucky fall. This is not so. Nature does not smile upon golf. Being inanimate, she is more apt to oppose obstruction than to further motion. The cleek approacher is consequently proverbial for grumbling at his luck. When the worm cast turns his ball, he is the worm that turns. Moreover, the trajectory of a cleek shot is so low, that the least shade of top will prevent the ball from rising at all, and then it will cling to the ground and go half-way. From an iron, a shot one degree too low is still in the element it was meant to traverse, not in grass, which has double as much resistance. 'But my cleek is as much lofted as an iron,' is what one often hears. No doubt it is. Most cleeks are. It is not the difference of lay, but of shape, which governs their respective lofting powers. A cleek, to loft as high as an iron of the same lay, would require to be thicker on the sole than they usually are, and as sharp as a knife on its upper edge. Even then its height of loft would be very uncertain. The change in thickness of metal from below upwards being so sudden, a microscopic variation in the height of impact would materially alter the amount of loft. In short, it is the depth of face, not the lay, which causes the difference in execution between a cleek and an iron. Certainly a more lofted cleek might be used. But such a weapon would in no respect be better than an iron, and would have the drawback of all laid-back clubs, a subject already noticed.

For approaching, the iron is on the whole the best club yet devised, and the one most in favour with players. It is supposed to be a very difficult thing to get a good iron. This is not the case, although it is very common to see men owners of, and proud of, very bad ones, which vastly increase their difficulties in approaching. This is because they set their affections on a wrong style of club. It is usual to carry two irons – a heavy for driving, a light for approaching. This nomenclature sets men on the wrong scent from the beginning. The two ought to be called the driving and the approaching iron, without this (as I hold erroneous) dogmatic reference to their comparative weights. Whether a driving iron ought to be heavy or light, or whether it ought to be carried at all, is a matter for individual taste to decide. But there is no greater mistake than to have a light 'light iron.' To say what weight it should be is impossible, so much depends upon the player's style and build. Roughly, it may be stated however, that an iron lighter than a driving cleek is simply a useless toy. Error in the direction of heaviness, whilst less common, would be less fatal. The lay of an approaching iron, as well as the weight, is a matter of importance. If too straight in the face, it either will not carry over bunkers and hazards, or else its owner will be led into a habit of jerking, in order to make it do so. On the other hand, a much lofted iron is very difficult to use. Unless the ball be struck with absolute precision, it either digs into the ground, or hits with its edge. A medium amount of loft is best. By merely looking at the club, it is impossible to decide whether its lay is right or not. An upright club for the same work requires more pitch than a flat one, experience proving that (as already insisted on) the more upright a club is, the lower its trajectory. Again, the thicker the sole is in proportion to the top, the higher it will send the ball. The proper way to decide whether an iron has the right lay or not is to try it. If a half-topped shot travels further than a lofted one over ordinary turf, the club has too much pitch; if the opposite happens, it has too little. However pretty an instrument, to whatsoever great man it may have belonged, reject it, and pick a new one out of a shop.

CHAPTER NINE

Of Putting

To the beginner putting seems the least interesting part of the game. It feels mean to go dribbling and creeping up to a little hole, whilst a teeing-ground, from which you may drive the ball unknown distances into space, is ready close by. The rabbits in the bents mock at it, rushing into holes of about the same size at headlong speed, and with perfect ease. Like other things, essentially foolish in themselves, such as preaching, pleading, feeling pulses, etc., putting becomes attractive in proportion to the skill acquired in it. The young player will tell you that he cannot putt a bit, as complacently as mankind in general compliment themselves on having bad memories. Not so the experienced golfer. His putting is a feather with which to tickle his lug.

That putters, like poets, are born not made, is a common fallacy which prevents many from becoming masters of the art. It is also a general opinion that to putt you only require to putt, and that there is nothing easier than to do so with the middle of the club. If you heel, toe, top, or draw a putt, you are accused of gross, wilful carelessness. The miserable man whose driving has gone wrong sets to work to amend his style. The putter at fault blames himself for not

Plate 19. Putting (1).

using his eyes more carefully, or else he gives up for the day, on the ground that his liver is out of order. There is here a fallacy. I do not say that one ought not to consider a semi-miss with a putter wicked, but it is not worse than the same crime with a play-club – nay more than failing to thread a needle is clumsier than missing a nail with a hammer. Nay, in my opinion, it is not so bad. Of the two, to hit clean with a driver is the easier operation. With the latter the main thing is to lay on. There are fifty styles in which this can be done, whilst, with the former, there are at most two or three.

Besides, for putting, a well-balanced club is absolutely essential. I am inclined to go further, and add that it must be made of wood. It is true that some hole out wonderfully with cleeks, others even with irons. But, by the shade of many a lost match, they are bad when they go off! Many men always putt with wood; few, never. The user of iron admits the inferiority of his weapon by carrying a putter to fall back upon when his fancy club fails him. I have just said there are, at most, two or three attitudes in which good putting is possible. I am inclined to be more dogmatic, and to assert that there is but one. The player must stand open, half facing the hole, the weight on the right leg, the right arm close to the side, the ball nearly opposite the right foot. To putt standing square, the arms reached out, is as difficult as to write without laying a finger on the desk.

The idea that a putt is merely a shorter approach shot is one which must be got rid of. Approaches are played with a swing, longer or shorter, according to distance. A putter is not swung, but passed over the ground. It is a common thing for a professional caddy, under special circumstances, to put an iron into your hand near the hole, and to say, 'Play as if you were playing with a putter.' Those who apprehend the shot know that they are to give the ball a sort of push. Many players, however, putt with a swing. It is necessarily a very short one, and they are popularly described as 'nipping their putts.' From start to finish of a properly played putt there must be no free play of muscle. The putter must be guided all the time it is in motion, as much as the artist's pencil in drawing a straight line. In time, and by practice, driving may become partly mechanical, and balls be clean hit almost unconsciously. You may become a driving but not a putting machine. Matter can be fashioned into a clock, but not into a portrait painter. It is because holing-out is a human act that none ever become infallible for even the shortest distances. Within narrow limits there is a choice of styles of good putting. It may be done entirely from the wrist, from the shoulder, or by a combined use of all the arm joints. It matters little which of these manners be adopted, so long as it is adhered to and persevered with in prosperity and adversity. But, however old a player you are, however good in other respects, if you are putting with a jerk or swing, a fresh start would be worthwhile.

A great secret of steady putting is to make a point of always 'sclaffing' along the ground. The best putters do this, although it is not evident to an onlooker, the noise of the scrape being inaudible. To be sure of the exact spot on the putter face which is invariably to come in contact with the ball, is, of course, essential to the acquirement of accuracy. If you play to hit clean, your putter must pass above the ground at varying heights, as it is impossible to note

Plate 20. Putting (2).

how much air there is between it and the turf. In the other way you feel your road. But the greatest gain from treating putting as a sclaffing process is the less delicate manipulation required when short putts are in question. At a foot and a half from the hole the clean putter often fails, from incapacity to graduate inches of weakness, whilst the sclaffer succeeds because he is dealing with coarser weight sensitiveness.

Although every golfer theoretically accepts it as politic to play for the back of the hole, yet few putt as if they thought it was. The majority treat the hole as a place more difficult to get into than it really is. They seem practically to believe that a putt one ounce too strong, or one hair's-breadth off the line, must be out. Consequently many short putts are played so timidly that they are six inches off the line, or within six inches of the goal. Now the fact is that (from short distances), the hole is pretty big, and from all distances it is capable of catching a ball going at a fair pace. I admit that more putts of over two yards must be missed than are held, because a putting-green is not a billiard-table; but many more would go in than do if players credited holes with a little of that catching power which they really possess. Someone says I mean nothing more than that a putt should be played 'for a foot past,' as the caddies advise. I do mean more. I object to that phrase. It should stand 'Play to be in and at the proper pace – namely, so hard that, if straight, you are in; if not straight, that you will be, not one, but two feet past.' With this faith in the hole, putts of a yard or under are very easy. Any pace between what will take the ball the exact distance, or two feet past, will do. Practically, in other words, the player does not require to think of the pace, and can give all his attention to direction. The putter who plays thus boldly has much to endure in the way persecution and ridicule. If, from a distance, he strike the hole and fall in, it is called a fluke. His short putts are laughed at as gobles. He is assured that had they missed they would have been out of holing. There are two answers; first, they do not miss the hole; second, if they did, they would only be out of holing for the dribbler who sneers at them. It is the inveterate practice of dropping putts over the edge of the hole which makes it necessary to discuss and study the line so carefully, and causes the power of calculating the effect of the minutest undulation or obstruction to be highly necessary. A man whose habit it is to play for the back of the hole at all times will seldom have any difficulty about his line. He will not require to crouch down and take note of obstructions which are scarcely visible. Anything that will turn his ball aside, and compel him to play with bias, will be visible to the naked eye. There will be no need to settle whether he is to take his caddy's line or his own – whether he must start an inch to the right, playing weak, or two inches to the left, playing weaker, or off the heel, or off the toe. Of course, it is very pretty to see a ball meandering into a hole, but, in most cases, it is quite an unnecessary treat, given gratis to the onlookers. Consulting with caddies has much to do with each putt being treated as if it were a thing by itself. If their advice as to the line and strength be followed, and the putt comes off, it is supposed (and they like it be be supposed) that there was no other way of doing it. Naturally, too, they do not advise the easiest way. A roundabout road is more interesting to them. And adds, moreover, to their importance. The simple-minded caddy, who always sticks down a pointer in the direct line between the ball and the hole, is credited with doing so from lack of understanding of lines altogether. But his advice is nearly always the soundest. Many players acquire faith enough to play for the back of the hole by using a cleek or an iron for short putts, and they then maintain that these clubs have the quality of keeping the ball true to its line. The putter will do the same thing if used with equal confidence, and that without the risks of either lofting or of those due to using an awkward, ill-balanced club, which an iron or cleek with its face turned in undoubtedly is.

If there are few who play for the back of the hole in ordinary circumstances, there are fewer still who do so when the only line is curved. If there is a moundlet which will cause the ball to diverge to the left, few go to the right just enough to make up for this. They set themselves to dribble the putt very far to the right, giving the unevenness of the ground as much say in the matter as they can. Anybody will play boldly along the top of a ridge when the hole is at the end of it, but most men prefer, to the detriment of their putting when it is on the side of one, to climb high up and drop down, to running quickly along the lower slopes.

In putting there is much to think about, and much more not to be thought of. With long putts, the great stumbling-block is the strength. Before taking his stance the player knows his distance from the hole and the nature of the ground. One glance more after he has done so is sufficient to assure him that he is aiming in the right direction. Looking back and forward between the ball and the hole will tell no more about the distance, but will only distract him from applying the force proportionate to it. For short putts which ought to be holed, the same holds good, except that starting the ball in the exact line is, or ought to be, now more a difficulty than the strength. Some fix upon a spot to play over before addressing the ball, others after; the most diffident get their caddy to point it out when they are about to play. But, however it is come at, there should be no hesitation. There is the line now for strength and accuracy. To take another look at the hole, to think 'Perhaps I am not aiming quite straight,' will certainly prove fatal. You will give an involuntary pull or push, or dribble hesitatingly up to the lip. But with faith in your line, your stroke delivered, you will look up and likely see the ball disappear down the middle – like a rabbit, perhaps, on account of the determined energy of your faith – perhaps by the side (a hole is very large if played at boldly), on account of some bias in the ground not noticed, and best unnoticed, but down all the same.

When a putter is waiting his turn to hole-out a putt of one or two feet in length, on which the match hangs at the last hole, it is of vital importance that he think of nothing. At this supreme moment he ought studiously to fill his mind with vacancy. He must not even allow himself the consolations of religion. He must not prepare himself to accept the gloomy face of his partner and the derisive delight of his adversaries with Christian resignation should he miss. He must not think that it is a putt he would not dream of missing at the beginning of the match, or worse still, that he missed one like it in the middle. He ought to wait calm and stupid till it is his turn to play, wave back the inevitable boy who is sure to be standing behind his arm, and putt as I have told him to – neither with undue haste nor with exaggerated care. When the ball is down, and the putter handed to the caddy, it is not well to say, 'I couldn't have missed it.' Silence is best. The pallid cheek and trembling lip belie such braggadocio.

CHAPTER TEN

Of Match and Medal Play

HAVING EXAMINED in detail the different kinds of shots which the golfer is called upon to make, a few remarks on combining them into a game may fittingly conclude this little treatise.

There is no such thing for the properly balanced mind as an uninteresting match at golf. Some greedy and ill-conditioned persons will not play in what they call 'duffers' foursomes' – matches in which the real flukes are the clean-hit shots, and the winning side that which has the luck to make the greatest number of these. On the other hand, there are dull fellows who will not stake their reputation on a serious match in which defeat means sorrow and victory joy, which classifies them as golfers, or decides the ownership of a five-pound note. The wise golfer who wishes his game to flourish will supply it with a judicious mixture of the two kinds – the friendly and the big match. A friendly match is the earnest golfer's holiday, and his opportunity for practising as well. It gives him time to listen to the singing of birds, and to observe the natural non-golfing beauties of the links. It is also his time for trying new clubs, modifications of style, or fancy shots which have been clamouring for recognition, more pleasantly, than in an hour's solitary practice. It enables him to set at rest questions about his thumb, the possibility of lengthening his driving, the advisability of taking to a cleek for putting, a mashy for approaching, etc., etc., all this, of course, without his partner knowing that his half-crown is being trifled with. But to play too many friendly matches is a great mistake. It is the direct road to a bad style and careless putting. The tone of mind during most games one plays ought to be an earnest, oathful desire for victory, which alone will fix a man down to the great monotonous essential of hitting the ball true, and distract him from the will-o'-the-wisp of style.

Games at golf ought not to be played for nothing, more particularly where adversaries are in the habit of meeting often. Glory may be a sufficient spur when trying conclusions with a stranger; but between friends there must be something more. If there is not, the worse player will not take odds, and the better, from having nothing to do, will fall back to his level. This trades-union, communistic plan of offering no incentive to skill slowly undermines it. But with a stake, the worse player will demand his odds, the better give them grudgingly, and both strive to win. 'What!' exclaim those who consider there is some mysterious wickedness in exchanging money for anything but perishables, such as food, drink, clothing, and shares in bubble companies – 'What! Degrade golf to a gambling game?!' Gambling! What nonsense! Is dinner a gluttonous and drunken thing because at it there is eating and drinking? 'I see,' says the tolerant moralist, 'small stakes. You would limit the betting to the "statutory ball" or equally "statutory half-crown."' Why should I?

Are there many cases of golfers crippling their resources by betting? Even if there were, who made us these people's grandmothers? Nevertheless the statutory half-crown has its merits. By adding up your collection of them at the end of the year, you can judge of your qualities as a match-maker. It is a fair criterion of your progress, or retrogression too. It has the advantage of being a uniform stake, which to wrest from your friend may be greedy, but is not cruel. From some people one might feel conscience-stricken when taking gold. It is unfeeling to crow when dormy three and the stake is large; but it is a fair game to jangle even half a dozen of a man's 'statutories' below his nose, or to invite him into a shop to see you spend them. Before we can do this, however, the money must be won. Attention to several matters will help players to win it.

It has already been remarked that excessive golfing dwarfs the intellect. Nor is this to be wondered at when we consider that the more fatuously vacant the mind is, the better for play. It has been observed that absolute idiots, ignorant whether they are playing two more or one off two, play steadiest. An uphill game does not make them press, nor victory within their grasp render them careless. Alas! we cannot all be idiots. Next to the idiotic, the dull unimaginative mind is the best for golf. In a professional competition I would prefer to back the sallow, dull-eyed fellow with a 'quid' in his cheek, rather than any more eager-looking champion. The poetic temperament is the worst for golf. It dreams of brilliant drives, iron shots laid dead, and long putts held, whilst in real golf success waits for him who takes care of the foozles and leaves the fine shots to take care of themselves.

If you have started with no other idea but to hit, in a short time it will appear that you are driving far. Take no notice of the fact. Regard the extra distance covered as anybody's business but yours. The greedy, grovelling spirit of the true golfer, anxious to win holes, is not to be beguiled from its purpose by the soul-satisfying, pocket-emptying glories of brilliant shots. During a match there is usually a great deal said about the state of the game, or the adversary's position in regard to the hole, and one is very apt to attempt to play accordingly. By doing so, many holes are lost which would not otherwise fall to the opponents. For instance, how often does it not happen that you are playing two more, and think it necessary to hole in less than the perfect number to secure a half? You make an effort, fail, lose a shot more; which shot, not the two more, it turns out, costs you the hole. Everybody knows that to press a drive will not add to its length; but it is not equally acknowledged that extra mental pressure for an approach or a putt is worse than useless. The supposed necessity for pressing is born of too much respect for the enemy. Because they have got the best of you for the moment, and played the hole perfectly up to a certain point, they are credited with being infallible. And you see no chance of their going into a bunker or taking four to hole off an iron. It is scarcely ever politic to count the enemy's chickens before they are hatched. Cases constantly occur of holes being lost because it seems absolutely necessary in order to save them to get home from a bad lie. Your forcing shot sends the ball from bad to worse, and what might have been won in five is lost in seven. A secret disbelief in the enemy's play is very useful for match play.

This contempt must, however, be largely seasoned with respect. It does not do lightly to lose the first two holes, or any hole. When one is down it is natural to hunger for holes, but even with five up play greedily for more – play a yard putt as if the match depended on it. Likely enough it will turn out that it did. With five up express, as is polite, regret at laying a stimy, but rejoice in your heart.

It is a great thing in a match to be one or two up, and to keep the lead. An advantage maintained for seven or eight holes almost certainly breaks down the enemy and wins the match. Yet everyone is inclined to be carelessly confident when they are ahead, and when they have lost their lead and some more, partly by their own fault, to apply themselves with undue and fatal earnestness. If golfers would but humbly acknowledge to themselves (which is true) that they lose heart and have bad luck when they are down, they would be more careful to husband their advantages. How men 'funk' is comically noticeable at the close finish of a big match. With all even and three to play, the side which can finish in fair figures is almost certain to win. But in these circumstances even first-class players generally give an exhibition of lamentable bungling all round.

Some particularly tender-hearted golfers play better in four-somes than in singles, because in the latter they are apt to have their bowels of compassion moved and their game made loose by the grumblings and lamentation of the adversary whom they gave got well in hand. Playing a foursome will not lessen his dread of the other side when down, but it will prevent the merciful man from being moved by pity. The wailing, the discontent about the odds, the deprecation of stymies, the harping on the flukiness of long putts held, his good luck, their bad luck, will not melt his heart and soften his muscle. Between him and them is one nearer and dearer – his partner. It is not selfish to crush the enemy; it is duty – duty to the partner. What are the tears of two enemies to the joy of one friend?

The choice of, and conduct towards, a partner are matters of considerable importance. If we get beaten, no matter who he is, or how he has played, or how we have played, it will, as a matter of course, be entirely his fault. During the match, however, it is politic to mask our disgust and contempt; for it is not the scolder, but the scolded, who is apt to go to pieces. No man who takes a partner ever questions for a moment that he himself is the amiable factor in the combination. This is all very well; but this belief in our own imperturbability often leads us to challenge along with some notorious grumbler, to play badly in consequence, and to lose. If we thus break down, we blame him, and unjustly. The fact is, our temper is proved to be such as to unfit us to play with a quick man. He has roared like a lion indeed, but played like one, whilst we have trembled at his roaring, been put out when he showed us our putts, sulked when he interfered with our shots or advised how to swing. It is we who have bad tempers, and should therefore choose perfect partners. He is qualified to play with either angels or devils, and win.

What is the ideal partner? He should be of a Laodicean disposition – neither too hot nor too cold, ready to utter one hearty groan over any gross mistake he happens to make, and then to say no more about it. At yours, he should show disappointment in so far as they affect the game, letting you believe at the same time that they were simply failures, not the results of vainglorious attempts – of selfish attempts – to do something brilliant. When you have bad luck he should sympathise; but fulsome falsehoods about the badness of the lie are loathsome to an upright-minded man. Gross hypocrisy on his part is only politic when you miss a short putt. This he ought to try over again, and miss. There are grave circumstances in life which make lies moral. This is one of them. A short putt missed may bring on a holing-out paralysis unless it is promptly treated.

The perfect partner, without letting you know it, looks upon himself as the backbone of the game, on you as the flesh which may err. He plods on whilst you miss – plods on still when you are brilliant. If you are efficient, he lauds you; if variable, he says nothing; if hopeless, he smiles and says, 'It can't be helped.' To him you are the chances of the game.

The perfect partner is not awed if you are exacting, nor sorry for you if amiable to his mistakes. If he is playing ill, he does not think of what you will say afterwards. He tries to recover for the sake of the match. If he be leader, he does not try to pull you through by extra brilliancy of play. If you are in a class above him, still more careful is he to attempt nothing beyond himself. Glory for the leader, duty for the subaltern. And if, perchance, it is he who is fighting the best fight, he is careful to hide his consciousness of this from his superior.

The perfect partner never volunteers information as to why you are playing badly, never suggests that you are taking the wrong club, although certain you cannot get up with it. He knows that although you accept a correction civilly, or even with hypocritical gratitude, you would not be human if you were careful to prove yourself wrong by making a good shot.

There *are* partners to be found possessing these and other virtues; but it is useless to look for one who, in recounting a lost match afterwards, will either forget your mistakes or remember his own. A perfect partner is what one desires. A perfect adversary on the other hand is to be avoided. To be regularly beaten is – Well! It is not golf, and it is politic to avoid or watch carefully those adversaries who have a knack of getting the best of it in every match they make. The two most dangerous types are the grumbler and the flatterer. The former begins by huckstering for more odds than he ultimately intends to accept, asserts that he is best in a foursome if a single is proposed, reminds you that you out-drive him, speaks about his liver, has a sore hand, or a sprained wrist – can't play in wind if it is blowing, in hot weather if it is fine, in bad weather if it rains. If you are wise, make a match irrespective of these things, or let him go home to bed. But the wariest are apt to be caught after winning the first match and lunching. They are apt to lose the next two by carelessness, believing what he says about being out of form. It is so difficult to judge of an adversary's play. Unless one is getting beaten off the green, there is a predisposition to believe that the grumbling enemy is not as good as ourselves, and that (if he is winning) he is winning by luck. If we are some up, and he harps on his bad shots, walks with his head bowed, only raising it to wail, there is a risk of his being treated as nought, and perhaps pulling off the match in consequence.

Flattery is still more dangerous than grumbling. Under its influence a level match for shillings may be followed by a round for pounds, giving odds. Out of the hundred shots more or less you have made in the round, the flatterer easily finds five good ones with which to turn your head. With putts especially he will succeed. A very straight or a very long drive may be used against you; but a few good putts are still more dangerous in the mouth of a match-maker. The drives – unless utterly given over to vanity – you know to be exceptional. But putts! Who doubts that on his day his putting is remarkable?

The adversary who out-drives us is not difficult to deal with. If he does so on the average, he naturally gives odds, a man's driving being the usual standard by which his game is measured. If it is only when he hits them that he drives far, he is still easier to deal with. Those who hit occasional screamers over-estimate their own game even more than the rest of golfers.

Judged by his apparent merits, the most dangerous man is he who is exceptionally good within the hundred yard radius. To estimate the comparative efficiency of men's driving is easy, but near the hole casual observation is quite deceptive. The faculty for occasionally sending the ball high in air to land dead causes a man to be over-estimated. He who, time after time, holes from a yard and a half is not necessarily a permanently dangerous adversary. It may be his own bad putting which so often renders these efforts necessary. If you are puzzled at So-and-so constantly winning, the key to the enigma will probably be found in the inconspicuous regularity with which he performs the apparently simple duty of holing in three off his iron. His approaches are not brilliant perhaps. It may even be that many of them are scuffled along the ground; but a close observation will show that they are invariably straight. Nobody is oftener past the hole than short, but the deadly player will have a good average of approaches finishing on the far side. In short, an adversary who does not seem to be playing his short game at all well, may be winning every hole because each approach is laid within fifteen yards and each long putt within fifteen inches – a very simple matter, which rouses no astonishment, but is perfect play nevertheless.

In match play, as a rule, it is the finish, in medal play the start, which is most exciting. In the latter, one feels how dismal it would be to drag round the links with an incubus of ten or twelve strokes too many for the first three holes. After one has warmed to the work, it is not so crushing, slowly, surely, imperceptibly to tail off. Successful medal play, however, calls for more nerve and patience than match play. So long as our card remains good, each shot is as important as the first, and as we near home with a good record the excitement becomes intense. Even from the last tee a carefully compiled and creditable card may be driven to the winds.

Some men give a very good account of themselves on medal days by playing a bold, gambling game, which either comes off, or requires three figures to record it. For him who is always there or thereabout, the medal round is too trying to be pleasant. Each shot is a solemn and difficult interview, on which depend momentous issues. After each there is a moment for thanksgiving, a moment of relaxation, a short walk, and to business again – to the business in hand. There should be no thought of anything else. The good medal player is no Lot's wife, ever adding up his card to see what is behind him. When he has to drive, he drives. Approaching, he does not see himself in the bottom of the hole in three; he only sees the ball which has to be struck. Visions of the calamities of missing do not flicker along the line of his putt. His round is dismal business, without reflection or anticipation.

Some golfers advise great caution in medal play. They advise to drive gently, to play round bunkers, to play putts for dead. It is not likely that the cautious medal player will have to tear up his card, or that there will be any double figures on it, but he may easily have a worse total than if there were one or two, whilst anything better than a moderate score is improbable. An easy shot is as uncertain as a pressed one. A flabby muscle is as little under control as an overstrained one. To play round a bunker is to give yourself leave to top – a permission likely to be taken advantage of, for the golfer's body hates to hit and loves to foozle; whilst his game is easily insulted by being made to go round, or play short of, a bunker, it ought to be allowed to try to carry. Besides, a bunker is not necessarily a very terrible place when you are in it. The player in one is as likely to win the hole as his adversary thirty yards further back on grass. Especially when the bunker is within forty yards of the hole is caution folly. A cupped ball on the grass is as likely a contingency as a very bad one in the bunker. The bunkered ball will likely be got out, whilst the same pusillanimous spirit which played the other shot may likely put it in. Besides, why should the bold player get in? To hit clean with a driver is not more difficult than to do so with an iron. In short, the bold game saves a shot if successful, and does not necessarily lose one if too daring. That timid play is a mistake will be made apparent on a moment's reflection to anyone who has ever entered for a scoring competition. He will remember having thought, 'If I go in there I am done for,' – how he has gone in, got out, and only at most lost a shot. Of course this argument only applies to ordinary bunkers. On every green there are some terrible ones – unfair ones, in which the punishment does not fit the crime. These must be avoided.

It is in putting, more than in any other part of the game that the would-be medal winners, and those who enter to see what they will do, are apt to fail on medal days. Bad driving, with a turn of luck, may lose you little or nothing; but bad putting runs up a score that you will only reveal to inquiring friends after one or two askings and some explanation as to what bad luck you had. Everyone starts for a medal a little shaky, needing something to picket his mind to, so that it may not wander away into realms of dread. In driving, one can prevent stray thoughts by employing the mind in keeping the eye on the ball; in approaching, one can deafen himself with 'Be up;' in putting, all formulae but make us more erratic. Any kind of reflection or moral resolve seems to put the delicate machinery out of gear. Resolve to be up, and you are too far past; to be dead, and you are short; to be in, and you are out of holing. Good putting grows like the lilies. In match play it is vigorous when the sun is shining, and fades a little as the prospect grows dark. But the atmosphere of medal play is either too hot for it or too cold. One wants it to save shots for the future at one time, at another to retrieve the faults of previous play. To putt well on a medal day, one must be careless; advice easily given, but difficult to follow until our card is hopelessly beyond the reach of human aid.

OUT OF FORM

A Chapter for Adepts

From the Badminton Golf Volume, 1890

HARDLY ANY athletic sport survives our youth. From most sports man begins to think of retiring almost before he has reached his full strength; but the golfer has not necessarily developed his best game till long after white hairs cease to be a novelty. There would be nothing phenomenal in winning one's first medal after tying with a son. It does not happen to be the case at present, but two decades ago all the amateur medals were by what the cricketers and football players of that day would have called old men. Again, many youngsters, no doubt, have won the professional championship: but there are well known men – Morris, Ferguson and Fernie, for example – who were past the first blush of youth when they began to beat all comers.

Although, then, there is no reasonable age at which improvement ceases to be possible or even probable, still, after a few years of play, whether we are to make further slight advances or not, most of us, 'for better, for worse,' reach a standard which is recognised as our game. We are sometimes 'off' this game, sometimes 'in' it. Besides this most golfers have an ideal game, the purified essence of their performances, the way in which they would play were it not for occasional missed balls. On this they base their calculations as to the number of shots they ought to take to the round. On this, with an allowance for mistakes indeed, but on the assumption that each of these will only cost one shot, they are handicapped and are entitled to win prizes. It is not with these occasional bad shots made by all, champions not excepted, that this chapter will deal. It has nothing to do with the fact that some players, and these not necessarily the best, are steadier than others; but with that common state of affairs in which a man decidedly and for some time continues to play a game which is below his average.

When a golfer goes off his game the reason of his doing so must either be due to some misconception or else to some fault in style; he either misguides or fails to control his club; he is, for the nonce, either stupid or clumsy. There are extremists who ignore style, who say the only thing to do is to keep an eye on the ball, and to compel it to go. On the other hand, there are golfers entirely given over to analysis. Even before they have broken down, a few more than the number of mistakes which are inevitable by any man, and which ought to be taken no notice of, serve them as an excuse for trying to find out some error in stance, grip or swing. But a little reflection must surely convince most people that their best game is not reached by plane alone nor by thought alone. Evidently, wisdom lies between the extremes. The stylist ought to remember that confidence, concentration, patience and accuracy are essential; whilst the man who knows nothing about his own mannerisms may suffer for forgetting that unless his club hits the ball in the right way his shots will not come off. Which has most

to do with our game, style or sentiment, is of no practical importance. A correct idea of which we wish to do, and a correct way
of doing it, are both essential. As it will be seen in the sequel that
I consider it best in case of a breakdown to seek first for a subjec-
tive cure, and only when that fails to search for a visible fault, it is
natural to treat the subject in that order.

Prevention being better than cure, the first question which
arises is, whether, having developed a good game, there is no way
by which a man can make sure of continuing to play it. The thing
is possible. If after a player was master of a club, he ceased to
dream of further improvement, thought no more of the matter,
became neither more careless nor more careful, took no notice
of his occasional bad shots, and (in driving) shut his eyes to the
length of his carry, he might continue steady. Not only is this a
possible case, but if not for a lifetime, at least for long periods,
many thus become masters of their game. Assuming all could
get it, is the steadiness so attained desirable? There is the risk of
thus securing what is not the best game we are capable of. This
is a sufficient reason for a negative answer, unless a man loves
winning matches better than the game. Besides, it seems to be
more than a risk. Although there are many whose each drive is
a copy of the last, this deadly uniformity is not characteristic of
our best golfers. The story of their rounds is a story of mistakes
and recoveries, of better play and worse to an extent one would
not *à priori* expect. Whether, therefore, it be a prudent thing or
not to set our hearts on repeating our average shots rather than
our best, to close our minds to all desires but that of flicking the

ball cleanly, it is not a plan for getting over uncertainty in play, which one is justified in proposing. Quite properly the general run of golfers from the best to the worst have a less pawky feeling towards the game. They wish to lose no opportunity of improving, and from overeagerness to do so they often break down. There is constant ebb and flow; but surely not necessarily to as great an extent as is usual. The history of a man's game is in most cases as follows. After a breakdown he plays humbly, putting in practice all he knows as to the elementary necessaries of a good style, and one day, to his surprise, he finds himself playing his game. This is the critical moment. If he would let well alone, continue to play with the same care which restored his form, and look upon each shot as an isolated result not guaranteed by the last, nor guaranteeing the next, he might remain master of his game, and have it to fall back upon when, say, a few days of hitting harder, or of attempting a more fanciful mode of approach, had proved unsatisfactory. But the usual course of affairs is different. As soon as he becomes conscious that he is playing steadily, the player gets out of himself to take a look at all the good things he is doing, so that they may be put in practice should he (which at the time seems improbable) ever break down. Having made a mental note, he proceeds with confidence. He ceases to bestow all this bothersome attention on each shot. Should anything go wrong, are there not the notes to refer to? He hits with freedom, imitates A's swing or B's stance, takes any liberty, and yet hits well. In a few days there is a crash, and he cannot hit in any way. It seems to take more than a lifetime to teach some golfers that, as a train will run a long way without an engine, so their game keeps on without care. They know the train will finally stop, and that even should an engine be hooked on before it does, that it will not immediately be going full speed. Yet if, after a few careless rounds their game slackens or stops, they do not see why it is so. Instead of attributing it to want of attention to individual shots, they look for some extraneous cause, hunt for it, lose patience, break down.

Without further illustration I wish emphatically to point out that many breakdowns, if not most, are due to ourselves and not to our style, and that many of them might be trifling, if we would but accept this fact. In most cases we will not. We want to do some harder thing than bathe in the waters of Jordan. We want to find some fault in style and correct it. To be told to do anything so simple as thump patiently, carefully, ploddingly, is an insult to the ambitious golfer. He wishes to be master of his game, not its slave.

Of course the breakdown may be due to a fault in style. How are we to know whether there is or is not one needing correction? Should friends to whom we appeal assure us they see nothing to account for our ineptitude, we may be sure that style is not to blame. Should no two point out the same fault, we may with equal confidence abstain from analysing it. In short, except when there is little doubt as to the fault, or as to it and failure being cause and effect (a state of matters which will be considered in its proper place), we should proceed as if our minds only were to blame, and submit to what the doctors call a course of general treatment. Contrary to what might be true in illness, general treatment can do no harm, as it really consists in what more or less constantly we ought always to be doing. General treatment means putting away all but the first principles of golf, and approaching the ball like a beginner. Perhaps it would in most cases be a good thing for the player to read over the elementary didactic chapter of this volume, and come next day to the teeing ground prepared to verify his grip and stance carefully, and to swing as cautiously as if he had never swung a club before. I do not, of course, mean that he ought to try a new style; on the contrary, he ought to verify the pet foibles in which he believes, as much as the orthodox essentials. He ought to revise the whole subject, working out the problems in his own way – revise it rapidly, which he can do because he knows it pretty thoroughly.

It is of great importance to discriminate between peculiarities which it is sensible to retain and those which should be discarded. One kind may be called natural, the other artificial. A natural peculiarity is part of a man's scheme for hitting the ball. His may not be a neat way of arriving at good results; but it is not a wrong one, because it has brought out the right answer. Of natural peculiarities a golfer is only semi-conscious. For instance, that which an onlooker would call a break in the swing is a feeling of slow back to the player; a straddling of the legs is his plan for standing firm; falling over thc ball gets his shoulders to work. There scarcely exists a good golfer who could not tell you of something he supposes himself to do which you would not recognise from his description. Artificial peculiarities, on the other hand – that is to say, peculiarities which are copies of the natural ones of some good player, or 'open sesames' of our own invention – consciously adopted, can never be worth keeping. They help us for a round or two to play better because they give confidence, and then either fade out or are discarded. For instance, the amateur champion of 1889 has a naturally peculiar stance easily imitated. Artificial copies of it are at this moment ruining many a man's game. His imitators stand with the left foot very much nearer the ball than the other, because this is what their model does. Having heard about it so much, this brilliant golfer is no doubt now aware of what his position is, but a few years ago he was not; and in answer to a question about it, he could only suggest that it was the means he had chanced upon to work out the problem of standing firm. That swaying of the body is precisely the fault this stance seems to engender in the swing of his imitators is a fact on which alone quite a chapter of instructive comments might be written.

When we have entirely broken down in our play it will be found in some cases beneficial to leave off the game entirely for a time. By doing so the bad tricks we have fallen into may be forgotten when we begin to take up the game once more. Being necessarily of recent growth these bad habits cannot be deeply rooted and may wither whilst we are away from the green. But unless it happened to suit their plans in other respects, few men would care to take such an heroic course. A similar advantage is offered however, by the long involuntary breaks in their opportunities of playing which are the lot of most men. These chances of inaugurating a better game ought to be kept in view by the returning golfer.

By whatever means we arrive at the tee with unprejudiced minds – whether the immediate golfing past is put from us by an effort of will or obliterated by time and other distractions – there will be no benefit if we assume there is nothing more to be done. In the case of undertaking a revision without leaving the green, that there is more to do is abundantly self-evident, and ought to be equally so in other cases. Yet it is very unusual for men not only to throw away the valuable opportunity absence from the links offers for recovery or improvement, but also to act in a way which ensures their playing badly. Because from want of practice their best play is impossible, they indulge in a few careless rounds, instead of recognising that if there ever is a time when a golfer can afford to play loosely this is certainly not it.

We now come to the second part of our subject, the detection and cure of specific faults. This is a delicate matter, but not so difficult as some think it to be. In regard to faults in style, it is impossible to insist too strongly on the necessity of remembering that to find them out and avoid them is not all we have to do. As on the one hand it is unwise too readily to try a remedy, so on the other our game will suffer if without sufficient trial we discard the remedy we have applied. The following would be a sensible mode of procedure. Try the correction, and if it succeeds you are a lucky man. If it does not, try another. If that too fails, it is midsummer madness to attempt more patching. Almost certainly the whole game is out of tone. Therefore, the thing to do is to go back to the first correction attempted, and keeping it and all the elements of good golf in view, to play a constrained, cautious, beginner's game, such as we have advised when the breakdown is purely sentimental – a game which feels stiff, in which the swing feels short, which we are convinced cannot enable us to drive a ball; but which in reality can, because the hands are firm, the sweep unhesitating, and nothing is neglected. If this care be conscientiously taken for a round or less, the player to his surprise will suddenly discover that he is playing his game. The recovery will not be sudden, but the player's attention having been given entirely to hitting the ball, the knowledge that he is himself again will burst upon him in a moment. The odds in favour of this being the history of the case are so great that it is scarcely worth while adding that, if it is not, the player must go through it all again, giving some other fault a good share of attention. The reason why such a course is almost sure to effect a cure is that when a man is not grasping at every straw, but really trying to discover his fault, he is pretty sure to detect the true one. Even should he have failed to do so, the fault which can resist the care he has been taking must be very firmly rooted. With these cautions we proceed to examine the principle faults into which men drift.

Whether in the case of a beginner or an old player, the ball when driven has a tendency to curve off to the right. There is perhaps nothing more difficult to get rid of than this form of bad driving; and why? Because it is assumed that when a ball curves to the right it does so always for the same reason, various terms for the fault not withstanding. Now this is not the case. A ball will curve to the right if the club reaches it with the face laid back, or if the ball is sliced, from either of these causes singly or from both together. It is very evident that to enable him to correct the result the player must know what is its cause or combination of causes. He must also get rid of the common fallacy that hitting off the

The picnic on the putting green – 'Just the place for it'.

heel, which often accompanies slicing, is a cause of skid. There is nothing more hopeless and heartbreaking than to try to get rid of this without attending to the slice which causes it; nothing more important than to distinguish between this and heeling, which is caused by a faulty aim.

If a man is only heeling – that is, hitting the ball from the neck of the club – it will not go to the right. It will only be foundered. If by examining his club the player finds that he is always hitting off the heel, that he slices some balls, founders some, and, above all, if he hooks a few off the heel, heeling is the fault that has got a hold of him. He may ignore the other results. They are each more or less occasional, whereas the heeling is persistent. When this is the state of matters the cure ought to be easy. He has only to be careful about aiming. Heeling as an isolated fault is, however, very rare; but it should be attended to at once, lest there come the temptation unconsciously to add slicing, so that the ball may carry in one definite direction and not be foundered.

Laying back the club and slicing proper send the ball to the right for different reasons. The former does so because the face is not perpendicular to the line of fire, but at an obtuse angle to that line. The latter does so because, although the face itself is perpendicular to the line, the club is swung across it. The faults are different, but the result the same. They both put a right-hand spin on to the ball.

When spin is put on the ball by laying back the club, the grip is pretty sure to be wrong. The player has his left hand too far round, and its knuckles nearly or quite out of his sight. This disproportion in the way of holding may be noticed whilst he is addressing, or it may be arrived at during the swing. The man who cuts a ball because of the lie of his club will usually be found not only to be gripping wrongly with his left hand, but also to be holding too tightly with it, and too loosely with the right. Although some good players allow the club a little play in the right hand, it is not necessary to do so. A man who is cutting ought to be encouraged to allow it none. He ought to aim at gripping equally firmly with both hands, and with neither hand more round the club than the other.

By far the commonest cause of balls spinning off to the right is slicing. There is a certain class of bad players who, persisting in gripping the wrong way, never hit the ball with a straight face, and consequently never drive straight; but as a temporary cause of balls flying to the right, slicing is by far the most common. We slice when, instead of sweeping along the line of fire, we draw the

'Oh! What a surprise!'

club towards ourselves across it. One reason we are so prone to this is that straight up over the shoulder and down again across the body is by far the most comfortable way to swing a club. None but muscles adapted to swift motion are called upon. In the true swing the club head goes back along the line of fire, and as near the ground as possible, by means of the arms, the rest of of the swing (till the club is away round) being largely done by the trunk pivoting on the haunches. Now the muscles which do this latter part of the swing back are not adapted for swift work; when used together with the muscles of the arms they are like cart-horses yoked to 2.20 trotters, and act as a wholesome drag on this too straight and rapid swing. One sees an analogous thing in rowing. At twenty strokes to the minute any tiro willingly 'gets his back into it.' But at thirty-eight strokes or more he would fain do all the work with his arms.

There is a misconception of another kind, which is apt to make recovery from slicing more difficult than it need be. To use Mr. Galton's word, many golfers 'visualise' a swing as a scythe-like motion, not as a forward sweep. They make the mistake of picturing a club as striking the ball in the same way as the bat of a cricketer who plays across the wicket. The feeling that the club head describes a curve along the ground causes men instinctively and almost unconsciously to allow a little for this curve, and what they visualise as its result – a pull. I am inclined to think that this way of misconceiving a swing and its result is accountable for the fact that, compared with 'heeling,' pulling is a rare aberration. Whether this be so or not, let the golfer who has been accepting this mistaken theory get rid of it, and let out boldly. It is at least undeniable that a freely swung club has no tendency to pull the ball.

Having cleared the ground of some misconceptions about slicing, the next point is how to cure it. Evidently, the time-honoured imperative 'slow back' ought to be taken into consideration. What is too fast back every man must decide for himself. The child whose natural pace is a run, the youth who still trots for a mile or two without inconvenience, and the man who has golfed all his life, can each, in his degree, swing more swiftly than a late beginner. We are swinging too fast back when the pace is beyond what the slow body muscles can keep up to. To make these work, to make it easy for them to do so, is the chief part of the problem of curing slicing. If a man is using his loins, he need have no apprehension that he is swinging too fast. But if he finds that he can quicken, and is inclined to quicken to an unlimited extent without inconvenience, the arms only are swinging the club, which either spins the ball to the right, or, its taking that line being prevented in some way (*e.g.* turning in the face), drives it weakly.

By altering our position (position, not distance) towards the ball we facilitate the swing of the body, and cure slicing. As the alteration to be made depends upon the way a man has of standing whilst addressing the ball, a word must be said on that subject. One style is partly to face the direction in which the ball is to go, and to lean on the right leg. Another is rather to turn the back to it, and put most weight on the left. There is, of course, a third style possible – namely, to stand perfectly at right angles to the line of fire. This stance may be ignored as not existing in practice. A compass needle swings on a point, but a human being inevitably emphasises his position on to one leg or the other. Which of these two classes is most prone to slice? There is little doubt that those who stand 'open,' and who have most of their weight on the right leg (the leg to which the other class must transfer it whilst swinging the club back), oftenest commit this fault. One can see why this is so. By exaggerating the position to absurdity, such a relation of man to ball can be arranged that nothing short of a half circle on the loins could get the club far enough back to do anything but slice. Whether or not to advise the player who stands 'open' to draw his right leg back and lean on the other is too revolutionary, it is, at any rate, the position from which slicing is most easily cured. Some people may think it has other advantages. In the days of feather balls, of light clubs, and narrow links little cut up by irons, neatness and accuracy were of more importance than power, and the open style therefore the best; but with the heavier clubs and heavier balls of today, a style which is more effective to force out of a cup is by many authorities considered better. If the slicer of the old school is not prepared to change his stance entirely, all that he can be advised to do as to his feet is to plant his left more nearly in a straight line with the ball, and to be on his guard not to bear too lightly on that leg.

The player in the modern style has more resources of this sort against slicing. He ought to draw his right foot further back and further away from the ball in proportion to the amount of 'skid' there is on his ball. As the matter is usually (and, indeed, correctly) explained, this lets him 'get his shoulders into it.' Golfers will understand that this is practically what I have called using the loins. How the moving of the foot acts in cancelling the tendency to slice, if still misunderstood, will be brought home to the reader by that most convincing argument, a swing with a club.

To shorten the swing is often effective against slicing. As there is much prejudice against this, and as it would cure not slicing only but many other kinds of bad play were it not for the reluctance of golfers to submit to it, it is worthwhile to try to show how mistaken the prejudice is. That it seems inevitable that they must shorten their driving is the reason why men would do anything rather than cut off a segment of the circle they describe. Most golfers have proved at one time or another by experience that doing so has lengthened their carry. But they look upon this as an accidental result of something else (they do not quite know what), and are persuaded that, in the end, their drives must be shorter. It seems

The Art of Golf

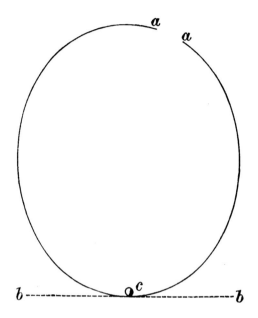

Figure 11. A 'small,' but commonly called a 'full,' swing. a, curve described by the club; b, intended direction of driving; c, the ball. This curve is classed as and called a 'full' swing. If classed according to essential features, it would be called a 'small' swing.

to them a very simple and incontrovertible piece of reasoning. There is a flaw in it, nevertheless. The flaw consists in regarding the completeness of the circle as the main thing, its size a secondary matter; whereas, within certain limits, the size of the circle, of which a segment is described, has far more to do with driving than the amount of segment. A consideration of the annexed diagrams will explain my meaning, and show why my statement is true.

The owner of swing No. 1 would call No. 2 a half swing,

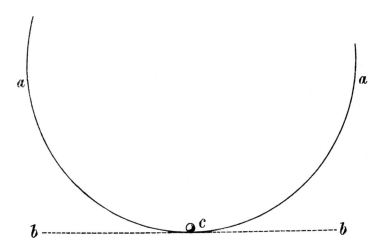

Figure 12. A 'big,' but commonly called 'short,' or 'half' swing. a, curve described by the club; b, intended direction of driving; c, the ball. This curve is classed as and called a 'short,' or a 'half' swing. If classed in reference to essential features, it would be called a 'big' swing.

although measured it is longer than his, and as a rule he would rather continue to slice than work his loins so as to allow his shoulders to describe No. 2, unless they were prepared to do the further work of completing the circle. Of course it is all the better if the club head comes well round; but that is of no moment as compared with the size of the circle. As in so many other matters, it is the loose use of words which misleads. It would be well, in the interests of golf, if the terms 'full swing,' 'short swing,' 'half swing,' were boycotted, and words referring to the size of the sweep substituted, such as 'big swing,' 'little swing,' etc., or, better still, 'flat curve,' 'sharp curve,' etc. So long as descriptions of style are based upon the comparatively unimportant fact of the amount of circle described, beginners and others will be misled, and energy wasted on what are, too often, meaningless gyrations.

At golf misfortunes seldom come singly, although we are taking them one by one. Whilst still in the miseries of slicing, or just as we are recovering, a fit of the costly vice of topping may overtake us. Before a hole is played out, a new ball may be nothing but a rolling mass of black grinning mouths, disgusting except as evidences that at all events we can hit hard. A fit of topping in the days of feathers must have been positively ruinous. To remember at such a time that it is not the top of the ball we want to hit, but a part of it which we can scarcely see, to remember this always, is not a bad thing. But this alone will not cure us. Topping is apt to come with slicing. When we describe too small a circle, swing too much up and down, there is only a proportionately small part of our sweep during which club face and ball will meet, a part still smaller if we draw the club across the line of fire, which we have seen is almost inevitable with such a swing. Although, mathematically speaking, a tangent to a curve touches it to a point, in golf they are practically in contact for an inch or two when the sweep is large; but if it is sharp this advantage is lost.

Topping, however, has other causes, causes which are independent of slicing. Men often find that for one reason or another they are driving higher than they like, and they try to prevent this by just a touch of top. If they would but think, it would be at once obvious that this is impossible. A ball is topped or it is not topped. There is no intermediate stroke. "What! No such thing as a half-topped ball?" is the incredulous cry at once hurled at me from the throats of several thousand readers. No! A ball hit to spout up cannot be made to rise the proper height by being also hit to 'dook,' except, perhaps, when it is hit from a tee as high as the club face is broad. Skying, for this cause, may be passed by. It is cutting from above downwards which makes a series of shots to rise too high, just as cutting across the line causes them to go to the right of the desired direction. If a ball is hit so as to give it the spin which makes it rise too high, topping or half-topping cannot give it a lower trajectory. When the swing is true, no matter the size of the curve if the ball is at the point where the curve touches the ground, the shot will be perfect. If the curve is large and the ball is hit as the club descends, it will have a little upward spin; if as the club ascends, a little downward spin; but in neither case enough spin to be of material importance. When the curve is a small one, the effects are different. The ball, hit as the club descends, will rise too high; as it ascends the ball will get so much downward spin as to prevent it (practically) rising at all. There is no time of hitting the ball as far as one can see at which half-topping will be effective. Therefore, get down to the ball always, and trust to a flatter swing to cure rocketing.

A consideration of the effect of cut upon a tennis ball will make my argument as to the futility of attempting to keep a golf ball down by half-topping, or, as some would say, hitting cleaner, still

71777

clearer. At tennis spin can be put on the ball by laying the racket back. Cut can be put on a golf ball in the same way. Bringing a racket down at an angle to the line of fire also spins the tennis ball. It is with this that we have to do. That the only way not to put a spin on the tennis ball is to meet it squarely cannot be questioned. The analogy is perfect, and proves, as I submit, that the only way to make a golf ball fly true is to sweep it from the tee as squarely as the manner of a drive permits.

A fear of breaking a club, or of losing impetus by striking the ground, are two other reasons why golfers top. Of the latter it is enough to say that a swing which will dig the club into the ground so as to check it, is so up and down that it would not be of much use in any case. Experience teaches that an honest 'sclaff' has no bad effect except, perhaps, when the ground is frozen, and the game cannot be properly played at all. Besides digging when the swing is too sharp, there are other things which prevent men from learning that they may sclaff with impunity. Hitting off the toe, and hitting off the heel, and turning in the nose, are all apt to break clubs. When, along with any of these, he also takes the ground, he is apt, very naturally, to blame the latter for the break. Taking the ground is, therefore, dreaded and avoided, with the result that topping is a constant trouble, till long experience has proved it to be not only harmless, but to some extent desirable.

Hooking is not nearly so common a fault as skidding to the right, because there is not the same temptation to push outwards across the line of fire as there is to draw the arms in. In fact, it is scarcely possible to do this much, unless when we intentionally force. As a rule, a hooked ball owes most of its spin to the club face being turned in. There are many golfers who have no occasion to guard against hooking. Those who have are, for the most part, persons unduly ambitious of long driving. Turning in the face keeps a ball down, and thus makes it go further. Standing far from it also lengthens the carry. Press ever so little when your club is turned in and yourself over-reached, and the hook is certain. Getting the right hand under the club, and gripping hard with it, helps a man to force, only at the imminent risk of the face getting turned in during the swing. To cure himself of hooking, a man has, as a rule, only to give up pressing. If that is not enough, it may be that stooping forward has become a habit he is not conscious of. The case of golfers who all their lives have had a wrong conception of the use of hands is more difficult. If you have begun golf and continued it with the idea that the right hand is a propeller and the left a fulcrum, you probably grip too hard with the former, and get it or both too much round under under the handle. Hooking is never far away from such a style, but to induce those who have it to change is scarcely possible. In spite of its crampedness, it drives a long way because it is a low ball, and anyone who has tried knows how hardly will a long driver be induced to give up his 'screamers', no matter how occasional they are.

The style of driving with the left foot nearer the ball is credited with being more conducive to hooking (and to wildness generally for that matter) than the old style. It is useful to remember that it is not the style of address itself which betrays players into fits of hooking, but a fault which it allows to grow. A man who stands open is made aware that he has got too far from his work by losing his stability and 'falling in.' Not so with the other style. He can overcome the immediate bad effects of stooping by increasing the relative distance of his two feet from the ball almost indefinitely, and thus getting his left leg as a prop. For the moment it is much easier to use this correction than to stand up. It need not be; but one can easily see that it always will be. Knowledge of this tendency will, however, guide the player to the proper remedy when his hooking or other wildness becomes so serious as to demand energetic treatment.

A nasty and not uncommon form of breakdown is what may be called general debility. We do not miss; we do not even seem to hit uncleanly. The ball rises to the proper height, and goes straight; but the distance is contemptible. For a cleek shot we need a driver. For a wrist iron shot a full one. When this occurs there is usually a sense of discomfort. We feel cramped and powerless. Our swing has neither beginning nor end, other than that we arbitrarily make for it. After a time we become accustomed to the discomfort, and do not feel it; but the golf continues as unsatisfactory as before. At this stage it is possible to detect that comfort has been obtained by giving a twitch after the ball is hit, instead of sweeping the arms away; and the player, if he observes this, sets to work to follow up the stroke. He finds that he cannot, and if he persists the discomfort returns. A follow up more vigorous and angry than usual may break a shaft over the left shoulder. He is a lucky man who grasps the meaning of this little mishap, viz. that he has gradually acquired the habit of standing too near his ball. I say gradually. Within a foot or so it is not of practical consequence how near or how far off the ball is. But if a man is continually at the nearer limit his style changes. Everything in his play, including the carry, becomes cramped and small. When the cause is understood, doing everything on a larger scale will soon effect a cure; not only that, it will develop a fine game; for to have persevered in hitting with the middle of the club through so much tribulation proves that the man's eye is in.

The player, without being too near the ball, may find his swing checked against the left shoulder if he is slicing badly, but the course the ball takes makes it easy to discriminate between two cases.

There is a class of fault to which the beginner rather than the mature player is addicted; although the latter is by no means safe from it. Until – and this may be for years and may be forever – a man is convinced that smooth swiftness and not violence make him master of the ball, he tries to get his body to assist him in wrong ways. Properly, the body must remain stationary. It must swing around as does the compass in the binnacle, but not as the boom sways about in a calm. At different parts of the stroke the weight of the body is transferred from one leg to the other, as a natural consequence of swinging, but any removal of the body as well as of its weight is wrong. One sways (*i.e.* moves) away to the right as the club rises, from a feeling that this is swinging, and that hurling the body at the ball is hard hitting. In addition to this misapprehension there is, in the case of the tyro, also the real difficulty of not swaying, which would all the more quickly be overcome if it were not the custom to teach beginners to rise on the left toe, instead of leaving that to the inevitable result of the body revolving in the proper way. A man who has fallen temporarily into this fault of swaying his body will find he is foundering his ball. He will be conscious of hitting uncomfortably hard, and will find, if he asks himself, that he is thinking of the ball as a heavy object. Let him reflect that drawing back and throwing himself forward would burst open a door, but would not send either a door or a ball more than a few yards. He will often be told that he is hitting too hard and that there is a limit to the power which is effective in driving. There is no such limit if power is applied in the proper way, but there are certain ways of applying force which are harmful.

The experienced player is not likely to fall into this way of attempting to drive so grossly as that it shall be noticed, but he is very apt to be guilty of an invisible form of what is practically the same fault, very difficult to detect, because as far as I know it has never yet been clearly defined and pointed out. When a ball is foundered, or in some other respect badly hit, the player usually accuses himself of forcing, swinging too fast, or not using his shoulders. There are many who have golfed through life with this stone around their necks. A laboured, forcing style may be suspected of concealing it. Often there is no outward indication, and only the player himself can lay his hand upon it. He can do so by asking himself in what sense he interprets the maxim, 'Let your body into it.' Properly 'let' here means 'allow,' not 'put.' An illustrative case will best explain what is meant. Suppose the driver to be swung back to its limit, it is the forearm alone (we are exaggerating so as to make the point clear) which swings it forward again.

The shoulders and body ought only to follow, neither dragged nor arresting. If at any moment the shoulders take the initiative the fault is committed. As a worm travelling looks as if a wave passed along it from head to tail, so the wave of muscular contraction for a golfing swing must pass from the extremities inwards. When the wave travels in the opposite direction, all the motions may seem correct, but the result will be unsatisfactory. Young Tom used to fall forward after a stroke. Many a bad player does so too; but the one fall is the very antipodes of the other. Young Tom let his body go with the club: the other pushes the club instead of swinging it, and ends by throwing himself at the ball.

Driving through the green may be passed over as being the same thing as driving from a tee, except in regard to one form of breakdown which can only originate in that part of the game, a breakdown caused by going to a new links. It is a curious fact that, although golfers are at most times ready to blame anything rather than themselves, when a different kind of turf might fairly be credited with a falling off one seldom hears that excuse. No doubt the links we are accustomed to vary with the weather, but its effects are recognised and soon mastered. Natural and radical differences between green and green, however, are not clearly recognised as a difficulty, or much angry thumping and disappointment would be avoided. To give detailed hints on this subject would take up too much space, without perhaps being of more use than the simple advice to golfers to be on the lookout for them. If on changing ground a man finds himself unaccountably 'off,' the first thing to do is to attend to its quality and to master its peculiarities.

For instance, many players find St. Andrews' links exceedingly baffling. The hills and hollows force themselves on the attention, as does the fact that to get out of the bunkers demands a special kind of skill; but that such beautiful turf is (probably from being much walked on) peculiarly hard is not at all manifest. Particularly if you have a 'sclaffy' style beware of the links of St. Rule. Taking turf there is apt to turn your club, or if by gripping hard you avoid this, there is a jar you cannot feel satisfied to endure. Being determined to get down to the ball, which is an essential element in your scheme of driving, you hit harder. The holes being long increases the temptation to 'let into them.' It is exactly the most unwise thing to do. What is required is to take the ball clean, which a more than usually easy swing helps one to do. But not taking turf, just as much as sclaffing on hard ground, inclines those accustomed to scrape along the ground to pull in the arms or else to sweep them round, to slice or to hook. These results we must avoid by taking more than usual care to follow up the blow with a correct sweep in addition to the careful aim. It is the quality of St. Andrews' links which makes their professionals recognisable anywhere. They seem to pick the ball off the tee as a bird picks up a seed, and to fly away with it, instead of tearing it from its place, which many equally good players from softer greens seem to do.

Under the head of approaching is comprised every shot – not a putt – into which the sense of weight enters as an essential element. To notice all the ways in which men try to master the problem of getting near the hole would not only be endless but also unprofitable, because, in addition to the vagueness and profusion in the terms used to describe approach shots, such as three-quarters, half-quarter, wrist etc., each player interprets these arbitrarily and according to a scheme understood only by himself and his caddie. I shall therefore only deal with the ordinary modes of approaching, however named, leaving fancy shots to those who trust in them.

Approaching differs from driving in that the club is not swung as far as possible, but drawn back in proportion to the distance to be covered. Accuracy in drawing back being the chief point, most men face the line of fire and play off the right leg, the position which best ensures accuracy, because it enables them to support and guide the arms against the body. It is a modern fashion to play off the left leg instead, which no doubt also gives the necessary support, but not so well: so that one is inclined to think that it is adopted in order that driving and approaching may be on the same plan as much as for any real advantage. To attempt approaching without emphasising the stance in one way or the other, or to consider that it is fragments of a full swing which are required, is unsound.

When an adept's driving leaves him for a season, it does not do so entirely. His slicing, toeing, heeling are not as grossly manifest as at an earlier stage. It is otherwise with approaching. A medal winner unable to hit with any part of his iron is no uncommon phenomenon.

Slicing is the most common and dread disease of both approaching and driving. What is true of the latter applies here, except that (even when one plays off the left leg) it is not likely to be advisable to alter the distances of the feet from the ball, but only the angle at which it is between them; because, accuracy being of more moment than power, the position is pretty certain to be already as emphatic as it can be. In which direction the correction is needed can easily be determined for both slicing and pulling, if here again it be remembered that it is possible to place the ball so far back that one must come straight down on it, or so forward that it can only be reached by clawing it round.

A cause of slicing which must be carefully watched is the taking back of the club. Instead of returning to the ball along the line it was withdrawn over, it describes a loop. This must evidently cut the ball. It is next to impossible to avoid making this loop or slightly wavering if our arms are free from the support of the body from the shoulder downwards, as they are when driving. The line can be kept if we draw the club back fast; but a quick swing instead of a steady withdrawal will make itself evident by general uncertainty in our shots. By one shot the ball is topped; at the next our club is pulled up dead, sticking in the turf. One shot goes high, another low. As for the cleanly hit balls, the distance they go is variable beyond conception. One intended to loft over thirty yards covers a hundred and lands in the sea. We know when this sort of thing is going on that our swing is too fast; but as soon as we succeed in withdrawing the club more slowly, every ball if not hit off the socket is sliced as badly as if it were. Why? Because to take the club back accurately, to control the distance it is withdrawn so that it shall be proportioned to the intended length of carry, we must have one arm at least down to the elbow rubbing against the body. To get this support it is not difficult to apprehend that we must play very decidedly off one leg or the other. The trouble is that often after this point is attended to the arms are still free, unless an elbow is wilfully tucked in, which has the effect of making us feel more like trussed fowls than golfers. This results because we are stooping too much over the work, instead of standing up, or because the hands are not pressed down, or perhaps are round under the club handle instead of over it. Even when these details are recognised it is often very difficult to shake into the correct position in which we can withdraw the club and swing it down again firmly without waver and without effort to a distance completely under our control.

Another cause of slicing is a too free use of the wrist. When it is the intention to play an ordinary approach shot – a shot without spin and without cut – the left wrist cannot be too taut. There is a wrist shot proper to which we shall devote a paragraph presently. A hesitating mingling of these two can only produce varied and undesired results.

When approaching off the right leg it is quite exceptional to pull, at least continuously. When control of the swing is lost we are of course occasionally erratic in this way as well as in others. But if pulling is the rule the player may feel confident that he is not pulling his club far enough back, and is making up for this by hard, spasmodic hitting. Approaching off the left leg he is more liable to hook. Indeed, it is almost correct to say that the fault being the same we go off the line in the direction of the leg leant upon. This applies to many faults but not to all. For instance, slicing is equally common to both styles. Hooking, again, is a certain proof of forcing, as we have just said, when the old style is adopted but is not as regards the new one. Whatever the style, the temptation to force approaches is very great, and needs constantly to be guarded against. It is recognised by most golfers that distance is most accurately measured by the inches the club is withdrawn, not by the amount of effort put into the stroke. It is not usual to play as if the opposite were true, but a compromise which is, if anything, worse, is constantly being attempted. For some reason or other measuring distance in the proper way is not natural, and unless we are paying attention, a slight degree of compromise slips into our game – so slight, perhaps, that the extent to which our approaches become less deadly is not noticed. By using a little more effort instead of swing, topping, getting under the ball, toeing etc., appear, and, lastly, when the swing has disappeared altogether there is a steady series of hooked balls.

Speaking of forcing approaches, we are face to face not only with a cause of breakdown when it becomes noticeable, but with the reason why, on the whole, approaching is such a weak point in most men's games. So strong is the inclination that it is exceptional for anyone to go a whole round without occasionally sparing a short shot or forcing a long one, although the practice is admitted to be wrong. The contempt in which that small class who deliberately use a full swing at all distances (regulating its pace) is held proves this. It would be well for golf if, when we laugh at this style, the lesson be taken to heart, and it were appreciated that a single length of swing is foolish for any two distances however nearly the same.

Doubtless a compromise with forcing arises sometimes from inability to regulate swing, because from causes already discussed the arms have no support against the body. But it is just as often because the importance of this matter is not realised. In proportion to their skill in other departments it is unpardonable that in the case of most players, holing in three off the iron without any display of good putting is not more the rule than it is. A golfer who does not from thirty yards get within ten of the hole considers he has made a bad shot. It ought to be equally easy to get as near from any distance within a hundred yards. It ought purely to be a question of inches of swing to mark off which a man could surely soon learn by practice.

To go out driving balls entails more walking than is pleasant, besides (unless one has something definite in view) being of doubtful advantage. But to practice approaching might be made very amusing. At the very least, whilst waiting for the adversary's arrival the time might thus be utilised instead of being wasted in aimless putting. A very conscious style may cramp driving, and thus shorten it. But it is of no consequence how far one can drive without a quarter shot. To know one's distances is here the essential thing. Approaching it is not possible to be too well aware of what one is doing. The stroke is not natural. It is not played instinctively in the proper way. In practising, after the player had seen that his position was correct, the point needing attention would be the speed and length of swing back. This speed ought never to vary, or, more correctly speaking (for the speed with which the ball is reached of course, varies with the length of swing), the force used should be uniform for all distances. After noting that the club is taken back and brought down again straight along the line of fire, one should learn how much swing is needed for different carries – learn this so accurately that it should be almost possible for each golfer to draw up for himself a comparative table of inches of his swing to yards of carry.

Approaching in the ordinary style there is one other point which requires constantly to be attended to – namely, the after swing. The length of this part of the stroke ought not, like the swing before the ball is reached, to be proportioned to the distance to be covered. Except perhaps for very short shots, which scarcely come under this head, the after swing must not be stinted in any way. Many of the best players make a point of following up the ball as much for all approaches as for a drive. You see them watching the result with the iron or cleek, as the case may be, resting on the left shoulder. If it does not come naturally to a man to complete his swing so entirely, he need not do so; but at any rate ought never to be lost sight of that clipping the after swing with any idea of regulating distance is the same kind of fault as, and has similar bad effects to, doing so before impact. It keeps the ball back, but, as with jerking before the ball is reached, at the sacrifice of all precision. In short, the distance to which the club is withdrawn is the only thing which ought to vary. This alone is quite enough to make a man master of all distances between a drive and a putt, provided there is no abnormal difficulty in the player's and the hole's position.

It cannot, however, be overlooked that there are many other schemes for dividing approach distances, which it would be shirking my task to dub fanciful and ignore. Some players are less ambitious, being content to attempt, say, three distances, for each of which they have a definite plan. Others, whilst looking upon three or even two distances are practically enough, are ambitious in another direction. Instead of being satisfied with one uniform height of loft, they aim at controlling their shots in that respect, using one plan or another according to the nature of the ground. When the chances are in favour of a ball with a normal trajectory being well treated during its run, they play it simply; when the ground is rough, they then try to make it fall as dead as possible. For short approaches there are weighty authorities that the distances are most easily controlled by loft and spin. They hold that what are occasionally called quarter shots ought all to be played from the wrist, with more or less spin, so as to fall more or less dead.

Whichever scheme of lofting, or whichever of the endless compromises, a man adopts, there is no doubt that he will be constantly breaking down if he has not very definite ideas as to what he is attempting. For want of these there is no shot in all golf which men are more constantly losing and recovering than the lofted approach shot. Whether used occasionally or always, at certain distances, the lofted approach is not a fancy shot, although many players have come to regard it in that light. They lose the knack, and not knowing what it is which lofts a ball, they have to give it up till by chance it comes back. The extent to which the heel of the club is pressed down, and the hands are over in the grip, is often relied on to make the difference between an ordinary and a high loft. Sometimes faith is placed in the amount of slice. The first of these (the heel down and the hands over) is a means by which the proper swing is facilitated, the latter is the inevitable result of swinging in the desired style. Slicing does not raise the ball, but one cannot avoid slicing when delivering the lofting blow. Holding tight with the right hand, and many other points which will suggest themselves, are in like manner not causes of lofting, but results of adapting one's position to the problem of the right swing.

To come to the point without further beating about, loft and back spin are the result of describing a small ellipse with the club, and not a large segment of circle. To do this the club is swung by the wrists. To let them work its heel must be down, and the hands over the grip. From the style of the shot we must slice across to some extent; but it is not this slice, but the slice from above downwards, which causes both the high loft and the back spin with its dead fall. If this required proof, Parks's new patent lofting iron would prove it, as that club was devised solely to obtain this back spin.

Being off one's putting is not a subject about which there is much to be said. Once understood, there are few faults into which players can drift unwittingly. If a man is off his putting, pretty surely the cause is mental. Patience, confidence, and unflagging attention are always required. Putting is entirely a conscious act, no part of which can become a habit. Driving may be to a great extent mechanical; but the nearer the hole we get, the less becomes our freedom, and, consequently, the intrinsic pleasure of hitting. To name the commonest faults into which men allow themselves to drift is all that seems necessary. Of these, jerking instead of drawing the club far back enough to sweep it evenly away is a very bad one. All the advantages of really, although not technically, pushing the ball are thus lost. Getting into any of the attitudes discussed under 'approaching,' by which the player loses the support of his elbow against the body, puts him at a disadvantage. Standing at a proper angle to the ball is of great importance. Men are apt to allow themselves too much licence in this respect, forgetting that in such a delicate operation it is not enough to be sure of hitting the ball clean.

No doubt some men are born better putters than others; but the very prevalent idea that for certain kinds of turf or for certain conditions of the putting-greens special faculties exist is one requiring a word of remonstrance. Till the strength required for a new kind of turf is understood, one may easily fail; but unless there is more required for successful putting than accurate hitting, to suppose oneself better suited for one green than another must be fancy. To get over being put off one's game by the nature of the ground, the thought of what it is like should be put away, and its keenness and tenacity alone studied. On the same groundless assumption of it being possible whilst putting to do something more than set the ball rolling at the proper pace and in the right direction, men seek to recover lost deadlines in the art by changing their club. Sentiment apart, this can but necessitate learning the use of each separately. To condemn the changing of clubs, it must be noted, is not to assert that there is only one proper club to putt with. Many good putters use cleeks, putting irons, etc. The fact that their cleek is better balanced, or their putting iron a better tool than their wooden putter, is a good reason for the adoption of one of the former. A badly balanced club is by no means to be overlooked as a real cause of going off in putting.